Hello, Sugar!

CLASSIC SOUTHERN SWEETS

Beth Branch

Globe
Pequot

Guilford, Connecticut

Globe
Pequot

An imprint of The Rowman & Littlefield Publishing Group, Inc.
4501 Forbes Blvd., Ste. 200
Lanham, MD 20706
www.rowman.com

Distributed by NATIONAL BOOK NETWORK

British Library Cataloguing in Publication Information available

Library of Congress Cataloging-in-Publication Data available

ISBN 978-1-4930-3363-8 (hardcover)
978-1-4930-3364-5 (e-book)

♾™ The paper used in this publication meets the minimum requirements of American National Standard for Information Sciences—Permanence of Paper for Printed Library Materials, ANSI/NISO Z39.48-1992

Printed in the United States of America

contents

In memory of my wonderful grandmothers,
Robbie Penn Heaps and Betty Gilreath Branch.
This book is filled with recipes inspired by their
creative spirits and loving hearts.

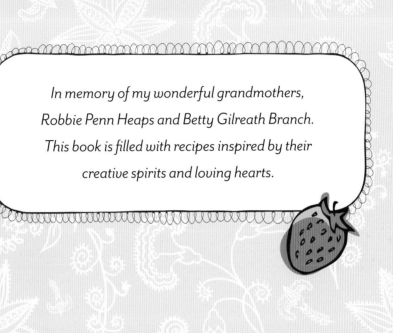

introduction

I have always loved baking, but I didn't really get into it until I was in college at the University of Alabama. As an English and creative writing student, I had been looking for a way to keep myself in the practice of writing often. I've always wanted to be a writer, to tell stories.

During my sophomore year, I began making ridiculous, over-the-top cakes for my friends' birthdays. I tried to create things that mirrored their personalities. A cake with a pie secretly stuffed between the layers. A sunflower cake. A boozy White Russian cake.

From a writing standpoint, I had never thought of creating a food blog. But my family urged me to make one so I would have a place to share my recipes and pictures. It's funny looking back on it. The decision to create a food blog, which was then called *The Collegiate Baker*, ended up helping me narrow down what I wanted to do with my life.

After I graduated, I decided to turn my hobby into a bit of a side hustle, and rebranded to the name Bethcakes. The term "bethcake" was the name my friends had given to the cakes I made. They would say things like, "I didn't know there was going to be a bethcake at this party!" I don't know that I ever told them just how special that was for me.

Over the eight years I've been blogging, I often wonder why. Why do I do this? What is the point? Why does it matter? And I have learned these three things:

1. Baking for someone else just as a kind gesture to make someone happy, is the best reason to bake something.

2. Creative outlets come in many forms . . . sometimes in the shape of a cake.

3. Life is about balance, but there is always room for more sweetness.

In a sense, I feel as if all of these things could be combined into one. Baking with and for other people is the sweetest gesture, literally and figuratively. You are saying "I made this with my hands. With my time. With my heart. I made this for you."

I've lived in the South my entire life. Southern flavors will always be some of my very favorite. In this book you will probably find some of your favorites too. But hopefully some will be new to you. I don't use cake mixes in my recipes. Some might have a modern twist, like Greek yogurt in place of sour cream or honey in place of sugar. Others will be the very definition of Southern comfort—all butter—even. . . shortening. Because some things shouldn't change.

Some of these recipes have been passed down through my family. I have a box of my grandmother's old recipes that she typed up on index cards with a typewriter. Someday I hope to frame them and hang them in my kitchen or over my table. There is just something so special about making those recipes—gifts that keep on giving. That is what I hope this book can be for you.

With love,

Beth

Cakes

coconut dream cake

A cake that tastes like a dream! The stars in this cake are the coconut caramel sauce between the layers and the fluffy cloud-like frosting.

SERVES 10

For the coconut caramel sauce:

1 cup granulated sugar

6 tablespoons cold unsalted butter, cubed

½ cup coconut cream

1 teaspoon coconut extract

1 tablespoon rum (optional)

For the coconut cake:

3 cups all-purpose flour

1 tablespoon baking powder

1 teaspoon salt

1 cup unsalted butter, softened

¼ cup coconut oil

2 cups granulated sugar

1 tablespoon coconut extract

1 (5.3-ounce) container coconut Greek yogurt

1 (13.66-ounce) can coconut cream (Thai Kitchen)

1 large egg

4 large egg whites

½ teaspoon cream of tartar

1½ cups unsweetened flaked coconut

To make the caramel sauce: Place the sugar in a medium saucepan over medium heat. Stir occasionally until the sugar begins to clump together. Continue cooking until the clumps begin to melt and turn an amber color. Stir occasionally until completely melted. While stirring, gradually add the cubed butter until melted. Gradually add the coconut cream until incorporated. Reduce the heat to low, and continue cooking for an additional minute. Remove from the heat, and stir in the extract and rum, if using. Let cool completely before using.

To make the cake: Preheat the oven to 350°F. Grease three 8-inch cake pans with cooking spray. Line the pans with parchment paper. Whisk together the flour, baking powder, and salt in a medium bowl. In a large bowl, beat the butter on medium-high speed with an electric mixer until smooth. Add the coconut oil and sugar; mix until fluffy. Add the coconut extract and yogurt, and mix until well blended. Add the coconut cream, 1 whole egg, and the flour mixture. Mix on low speed until mostly combined and then medium speed until completely combined.

Place the egg whites in a medium bowl and beat on medium speed with an electric mixer until foamy. Add the cream of tartar and continue mixing until stiff peaks form. Fold the meringue and flaked coconut into the cake batter until completely incorporated. Divide the batter evenly among the cake pans, and bake 28–30 minutes, or until a toothpick inserted into the center of the cake comes out clean. Let the cakes cool in the pans for 10 minutes, then transfer to a wire rack to cool completely.

To make the frosting: In a large bowl, beat the butter on medium speed until smooth. Add the shortening, and mix until creamy. Add the extract, confectioners' sugar, and coconut cream. Mix on low speed until mostly combined, then medium-high speed until completely combined.

For the coconut buttercream:

1 cup butter, softened

1 cup vegetable shortening

2 tablespoons coconut extract

6 cups confectioners' sugar

1–2 tablespoons coconut cream (or regular whole milk)

For the garnishes:

Coconut

Toasted coconut

Any remaining caramel sauce

To assemble cake: Place one cake layer on a cake plate. Pipe a ring of frosting around the top edge of the cake layer to build a barrier. Fill with caramel sauce. Place another layer on top. Repeat the process with frosting and caramel. Place the final layer on top. Spread frosting around the outside of the cake. Press shredded or toasted coconut all over the cake to garnish. Serve with any remaining caramel sauce.

lemon-blueberry cornbread cake
with Honey-Buttermilk Glaze

Baked in a cast-iron skillet, this cornbread cake is the perfect snack with a cup of coffee or a glass of tea. It's full of fresh, springtime flavor and has a sweet buttermilk glaze to top it all off.

SERVES 10

For the lemon-blueberry cornbread cake:

½ cup unsalted butter, melted

½ cup granulated sugar

¼ cup packed light brown sugar

1 lemon, zested and juiced

1 teaspoon lemon extract

2 large eggs

¾ cup buttermilk

1¼ cups all-purpose flour

1 cup yellow cornmeal

2 teaspoons baking powder

Pinch of salt

1¼ cups fresh blueberries

For the honey-buttermilk glaze:

¾ cup confectioners' sugar

2 tablespoons honey

2 tablespoons buttermilk

To make the cake: Preheat the oven to 350°F. Grease a 9-inch cast-iron skillet with oil. Combine the butter, both sugars, lemon zest and juice, and extract in a medium bowl. Mix on medium speed with an electric mixer until well blended. Add the eggs, and mix well. Next, add the buttermilk, flour, cornmeal, baking powder, and salt. Mix until all of the ingredients are incorporated. Fold in the blueberries.

Pour the batter into the prepared skillet. Bake 23–25 minutes, or until the cake is golden brown and a toothpick inserted into the center comes out clean.

To make the glaze: While the cake is cooling, whisk together the confectioners' sugar, honey, and buttermilk until smooth. Pour the glaze over the warm cake, which is best served slightly warm.

red velvet cake
with Caramel–Cream Cheese Frosting

This cake is a Southern classic with a fun twist! Because of the cake's light cocoa flavor, caramel is the perfect addition to the silky cream cheese frosting.

SERVES 10

For the red velvet cake:

2¾ cups all-purpose flour

1½ tablespoons unsweetened cocoa powder

1½ teaspoons baking soda

½ teaspoon salt

2 cups granulated sugar

1 cup vegetable oil

2 teaspoons vanilla extract

1 tablespoon white vinegar

3 eggs

1¼ cups buttermilk

½ tablespoon red gel food coloring

For the caramel cream cheese frosting:

1 (8-ounce) package cream cheese, room temperature

½ cup butter, room temperature

¼ cup caramel sauce

1 tablespoon vanilla extract

5 cups confectioners' sugar

For the garnishes:

Cake crumbs

Cocoa powder

Caramel sauce

To make the cake: Preheat the oven to 350°F. Line two 8-inch cake pans with parchment paper, and spray with cooking spray. In a medium bowl, whisk together the flour, cocoa powder, baking soda, and salt; set aside. Combine the sugar, oil, vanilla, and vinegar in a large bowl. Mix with an electric mixer on medium speed until blended. Add the eggs and mix well.

Add half of the buttermilk and half of the flour mixture. Mix until the ingredients are mostly combined. Repeat with the remaining buttermilk and flour. Stir in the food coloring.

Divide the batter evenly between the prepared pans, and bake for 25 minutes, or until a toothpick inserted into the center of each cake layer comes out clean. Let the cakes cool in the pans for 10 minutes, and then transfer to a wire rack to cool completely.

To make the frosting: In a large bowl, beat the cream cheese on medium-high speed with an electric mixer until smooth. Add the butter and caramel; mix until incorporated. Add the vanilla and confectioners' sugar. Mix on low speed until mostly combined, and then medium-high speed until completely combined and fluffy.

To assemble: Place one cake layer on a cake plate. Spread the frosting over cake, and top with the second cake layer. Spread the frosting over the outside of the cake. Garnish with cake crumbs or cocoa powder, or drizzle with caramel sauce.

kentucky butter cake
with Bourbon Whipped Cream and Berries

One bite of this cake will transport you straight to bourbon country! The cake is drizzled with a bourbon soak while it's still warm from the oven. Serve it with a dollop of whipped cream and your favorite fresh berries.

SERVES 12

For the Kentucky butter cake:

3 cups all-purpose flour

1 teaspoon baking powder

½ teaspoon baking soda

1 teaspoon salt

1 cup butter, room temperature

2 cups granulated sugar

1 tablespoon vanilla bean paste (or use vanilla extract)

4 large eggs

1 cup buttermilk

For the bourbon soak:

½ cup bourbon

¼ cup water

¼ cup granulated sugar

For the bourbon whipped cream:

1½ cups heavy whipping cream

3 tablespoons confectioners' sugar

2 tablespoons bourbon

For the garnishes:

Confectioners' sugar

Fresh berries

Mint (optional)

Honey (optional)

To make the cake: Preheat the oven to 350°F. Spray a 12-cup Bundt pan with cooking spray. In a medium bowl, whisk together the flour, baking powder, baking soda, and salt. Set aside. Cream the butter with an electric mixer on medium-high speed until smooth in a large bowl. Add the sugar and vanilla; mix until fluffy. Add the eggs, and mix until just combined. Add the flour mixture and buttermilk. Mix until well blended. Pour the batter into the prepared pan, and bake 45–50 minutes, or until the cake is golden brown and a toothpick inserted into the center comes out clean.

To make the bourbon soak: Combine the bourbon, water, and sugar in a small saucepan over medium heat. Stir gently until the sugar has dissolved. Continue cooking until the mixture is reduced by half. Remove from the heat. Use a toothpick to poke holes all over the cake in the Bundt pan. Drizzle the bourbon soak over the cake, and let it sit until the cake is cool.

To make the bourbon whipped cream: Whip the heavy cream in the bowl of a stand mixer fitted with the whisk attachment. While the mixer is running, add the confectioners' sugar and bourbon. Whip until stiff peaks form.

To serve: Invert the cake onto a cake plate. Dust with confectioners' sugar. Serve with bourbon whipped cream and garnish with fresh berries, mint, and drizzles of honey if desired.

mint julep cupcakes

Turn your favorite Southern cocktail into your new favorite cupcakes! The mint julep flavor comes from bourbon frosting and a sprinkle of mint sugar for garnish.

MAKES 24

For the mint sugar:

½ cup granulated sugar

2 tablespoons packed light brown sugar

3 large fresh mint leaves

For the cupcakes:

2½ cups all-purpose flour

1 tablespoon baking powder

½ teaspoon salt

½ cup canola oil

1¼ cups granulated sugar

¼ cup packed light brown sugar

3 large eggs

1 teaspoon vanilla extract

1¼ cups buttermilk

¼ cup bourbon

For the bourbon buttercream:

½ cup bourbon

1 cup butter, softened

1 cup vegetable shortening

6 cups confectioners' sugar

1 teaspoon vanilla extract

For the garnishes:

Pearl sprinkles

Mint sugar

Fresh mint leaves

To make the mint sugar: Combine all of the ingredients in a food processor. Process until the mint leaves are evenly mixed throughout the sugar. Set aside.

To make the cupcakes: Preheat the oven to 350°F. Line two 12-cup muffin pans with paper liners. Whisk together the flour, baking powder, and salt in a medium bowl. Set aside. In a large bowl, combine the oil, both sugars, eggs, and vanilla. Mix on medium speed with an electric mixer until combined. Add the buttermilk and flour mixture; mix until well blended.

Spoon the batter into the paper liners, filling until they are about two-thirds full. Bake 23–25 minutes, or until the cupcakes are golden brown and set in the center. Remove from the oven, and brush the bourbon over the top of each cupcake. Let the cupcakes cool completely.

To make the frosting: Heat the bourbon in a small saucepan over medium heat until simmering. Simmer until the liquid is reduced by half and measures ¼ cup. Let cool completely. In a large bowl, cream the butter on medium-high speed with an electric mixer until smooth. Add the shortening and mix well. Next, add the confectioners' sugar, vanilla, and cooled bourbon reduction. Mix on low speed until mostly combined, and then medium-high speed until completely combined and the frosting is fluffy.

To serve: Pipe the frosting onto the cooled cupcakes. Garnish with sprinkles, mint sugar, and mint leaves.

orange chiffon cake
with Sweet Beer Glaze

I'll admit that I'm not much of a beer drinker, but I'm all for it when it's combined with citrus and fruity flavors. This fluffy chiffon cake is flavored with fresh orange juice and zest and then topped with a sweetened, citrusy beer glaze.

SERVES 12

For the orange chiffon cake:

2¼ cups cake flour

1½ cups granulated sugar

1 tablespoon baking powder

½ teaspoon salt

½ cup vegetable oil

¾ cup orange juice

6 large eggs, yolks and whites separated

2 tablespoons orange zest

1 teaspoon vanilla extract

1 teaspoon cream of tartar

For the sweet beer glaze:

1 cup confectioners' sugar

2–3 tablespoons citrus-flavored beer

For the garnishes (optional):

Orange zest

Dried orange slices

To make the cake: Preheat the oven to 350°F. Spray an angel food cake pan with cooking spray. Whisk together the cake flour, sugar, baking powder, and salt in a large bowl. Add the vegetable oil, orange juice, and egg yolks. Mix on medium speed with an electric mixer until completely incorporated. Add the orange zest and vanilla extract, and mix well.

In a large bowl, add the egg whites and cream of tartar. Mix on medium-high speed until stiff peaks form. Fold half of the meringue into the cake batter, and then repeat with the second half.

Pour the batter into the prepared cake pan. (The cake pan should be about two-thirds full.) Place the pan on a baking sheet, and bake for 45 minutes, or until a toothpick inserted into the cake comes out clean. Let the cake cool 10–15 minutes before inverting onto a cooling rack. Let the cake cool completely.

To make the glaze: Whisk together the confectioners' sugar and beer.

To assemble the cake: Drizzle the glaze over the cake. Garnish with orange zest and dried orange slices. Fresh or candied orange slices work just as well if desired.

pumpkin cinnamon roll cake

This cake is your cup of coffee's new best friend, preferably enjoyed on a crisp autumn morning or afternoon.

SERVES 8

For the cake:

2 cups all-purpose flour

1 teaspoon baking powder

½ teaspoon baking soda

½ teaspoon salt

½ teaspoon pumpkin
   pie spice

½ cup butter, softened

⅔ cup granulated sugar

2 large eggs

1 teaspoon vanilla extract

1 cup canned pumpkin
   puree

½ cup whole milk

For the cinnamon swirl:

3 tablespoons butter, melted

4 tablespoons packed light
   brown sugar

2 teaspoons cinnamon

For the glaze:

1 cup confectioners' sugar

4 tablespoons whole milk

To make the cake: Preheat the oven to 350°F. Spray a 9-inch spring-form pan with nonstick cooking spray. Wrap aluminum foil around the bottom and up the sides of the pan to prevent leaking. In a medium bowl, whisk together the flour, baking powder, baking soda, salt, and pumpkin pie spice in a bowl. Set aside.

Cream the butter on medium-high speed with an electric mixer until smooth. Add the sugar, and beat until fluffy. Add the eggs, vanilla, and pumpkin puree; mix well. Add the milk and the flour mixture. Mix until well blended. Pour the batter into the prepared pan.

To create the cinnamon swirl: Stir together the butter, brown sugar, and cinnamon in a small bowl. Transfer the mixture to a squeeze bottle or a piping bag with a small tip cut off. Pipe the cinnamon mixture in a large swirl over the cake batter.

Place the springform pan on a baking sheet, and bake 45–50 minutes, or until the center of the cake has set and a toothpick inserted into the center (avoid the cinnamon swirl) comes out clean. Let the cake cool in the pan.

To make the glaze: Whisk together the confectioners' sugar and milk in a small bowl.

To assemble the cake: Drizzle the glaze over the cake while the cake is still slightly warm. Slice and serve.

hummingbird cupcakes
with Browned Butter Frosting and Pineapple Flowers

It's no secret that Hummingbird Cake is a Southern staple when it comes to desserts. Here it's paired with a slightly more modern frosting and garnished with dried pineapple flowers, which are much easier to make than they look!

MAKES 24

For the dried pineapple flowers:

2 pineapples

For the hummingbird cupcakes:

3 cups all-purpose flour

1 teaspoon baking soda

1 teaspoon baking powder

1½ teaspoons ground cinnamon

1 teaspoon salt

1 cup mashed banana (about 2 large, ripe bananas)

1 (8-ounce) can crushed pineapple in juice, drained

¼ cup honey

1¾ cups granulated sugar

2 teaspoons vanilla extract

1 cup canola or vegetable oil

¼ cup whole milk

3 large eggs

¾ cup chopped pecans

To make the dried pineapple flowers: Preheat the oven to 225°F. Cut the top and bottom from each pineapple. Peel the pineapples, and use a melon baller to remove any eyes/seeds remaining in the flesh. Thinly slice the pineapple using a sharp knife or mandolin. Lay the slices on a couple sheets of paper towels, and press with more paper towels to soak up as much of the liquid as possible. Arrange the slices on parchment paper–lined baking sheets, and bake for 30 minutes. Flip the slices over, and bake another 30 minutes. The pineapple should shrink slightly and be completely dry. If not, continue baking in 5- to 10-minute increments until dry. Immediately lay the pineapple slices in the muffin pans so that the petals curve upward like a flower. Let the pineapple flowers dry and firm up overnight.

To make the cupcakes: Preheat the oven to 350°F. Line two muffin pans with paper liners. In a medium bowl, whisk together the flour, baking soda, baking powder, ground cinnamon, and salt. In a large bowl, combine the banana, crushed pineapple, honey, sugar, vanilla, oil, and milk. Mix on medium speed with an electric mixer until blended. Add the eggs and mix well. Add the flour mixture, and mix on low speed until mostly combined, and then on medium speed until completely combined. Fold in the pecans. Spoon the cake batter into the paper liners, filling each about three-quarters full. Bake for 15 minutes, or until the tops are golden brown and the centers have set. Let the cupcakes cool in the pans for 5–10 minutes, then remove to a wire rack to cool completely.

To make the frosting: Place the butter in a small, light-colored saucepan over medium heat. Melt the butter, swirling the pot occasionally. Bring to a simmer, and let cook until the butter begins to turn amber and smells nutty. Browned bits of butter should be visible in the bottom of the pot. Remove from the heat and cool completely.

For the browned butter frosting:

1 cup butter

1 cup vegetable shortening

1 teaspoon vanilla extract

6 cups confectioners' sugar

2 tablespoons whole milk

Transfer to the refrigerator until firm. (This process can be done a day or two in advance. Store the browned butter covered in the refrigerator.)

In a large bowl, beat the browned butter on medium-high speed with an electric mixer until smooth. Add the shortening, and mix until incorporated. Add the vanilla and half of the confectioners' sugar. Mix on low speed until mostly combined, then on medium-high speed until completely combined. Repeat with the second half of the confectioners' sugar and the milk.

To serve: Pipe or spread the frosting onto the cooled cupcakes. Garnish with pineapple flowers.

marbled brown sugar pound cake

You can't go wrong with brown sugar pound cake and chocolate pound cake swirled together in one Bundt pan. The trick for marbled cakes is to use a knife or wooden pick and slowly move it in an up-and-down motion through the center of the cake batter.

SERVES 12

For the cake:

1 cup butter, softened

2 cups packed light brown sugar

5 large eggs

¼ cup canola oil

1 tablespoon vanilla extract

3 cups all-purpose flour

1 teaspoon baking powder

½ teaspoon baking soda

Pinch of ground cinnamon

½ teaspoon salt

1 cup plus 2 tablespoons whole milk, divided

3 tablespoons cocoa powder

For the brown sugar glaze:

½ cup butter

½ cup packed light brown sugar

¼ cup whole milk

2 teaspoons vanilla extract

Pinch of salt

2½ cups confectioners' sugar

For the garnish:

Chopped, toasted pecans

To make the cake: Preheat the oven to 350°F. Spray a Bundt cake pan with cooking spray.

In a large bowl, cream the butter on medium-high speed with an electric mixer until smooth. Add the brown sugar and mix until fluffy. Add the eggs, oil, and vanilla, mixing until well blended. Next, add the flour, baking powder, baking soda, cinnamon, salt, and 1 cup milk. Mix until combined.

Remove 2 cups of the cake batter into a separate medium bowl. Add the cocoa powder and 2 tablespoons milk; stir until incorporated.

Spoon half of the brown sugar cake batter into the prepared Bundt cake pan. Spoon half of the chocolate cake batter on top, spreading to the edges of the pan. Repeat layers with the remaining brown sugar and chocolate cake batter.

To create the marbled effect: Run a knife through the center of the batter once, moving the knife up and down slowly. Bake 45–50 minutes, or until a toothpick inserted into the center of the cake comes out clean. Let the cake cool in the pan 10–15 minutes before inverting onto a wire rack to cool completely.

To make the glaze: Melt the butter in a medium saucepan over medium heat. Add the brown sugar and stir until it has dissolved, about 2 minutes. Add the milk and bring the mixture to a boil; remove from the heat. Whisk in the vanilla, salt, and confectioners' sugar until smooth. Drizzle the glaze over the cooled cake. Sprinkle with pecans.

apple cinnamon crumb loaf

Apple lovers, this one's for you! This little loaf is loaded with apples, swirls of cinnamon, and plenty of crunchy crumb topping.

SERVES 8

For the crumbs:

⅓ cup all-purpose flour

⅓ cup packed light brown sugar

½ teaspoon ground cinnamon

3 tablespoons butter

For the apple cinnamon loaf:

⅓ cup packed light brown sugar

2 teaspoons ground cinnamon, divided

½ cup butter, softened

¾ cup granulated sugar

2 large eggs

2 teaspoons vanilla extract

1½ cups all-purpose flour

2 teaspoons baking powder

¾ cup whole milk

2 cups peeled and diced apples

To make the crumbs: Combine the flour, brown sugar, and cinnamon. Add the butter and use a pastry cutter or fork to cut it into the dry ingredients until the mixture is crumbly.

To make the loaf: Preheat the oven to 350°F. Spray a 9 X 5-inch loaf pan with cooking spray.

Stir together the brown sugar and 1 teaspoon cinnamon in a small bowl. Set aside.

In a large bowl, combine the butter and granulated sugar. Mix on medium speed with an electric mixer until fluffy. Add the eggs and vanilla; mix well. Next add the flour, baking powder, and milk. Mix until well blended.

Stir together the apples and the remaining 1 teaspoon cinnamon. Layer half of the batter, half of the apples, and half of the brown sugar mixture. Repeat layers once. Sprinkle the top with crumbs. Bake 50–55 minutes, or until a toothpick inserted into the center comes out mostly clean. Let the cake cool slightly; serve warm.

lemon–cream cheese pound cake

The only thing that could possibly make a lemony loaf of pound cake better is definitely a swirl of cream cheese through the middle!

SERVES 8

For the cream cheese filling:

1 (8-ounce) package cream cheese

¼ cup granulated sugar

1 large egg

½ teaspoon vanilla extract

For the lemon pound cake:

1½ cups all-purpose flour

2 teaspoons baking powder

½ teaspoon salt

1 cup granulated sugar

3 large eggs

½ cup vegetable or canola oil

4 ounces plain Greek yogurt

1 tablespoon lemon extract

2 tablespoons lemon zest

For the glaze:

½ cup confectioners' sugar

2–3 tablespoons lemon juice

To make the filling: In a medium bowl, beat the cream cheese on medium speed with an electric mixer until smooth. Add the sugar, egg, and vanilla. Mix until well blended; set aside.

To make the cake: Preheat the oven to 350°F. Line a 9 X 5-inch loaf pan with aluminum foil, leaving enough overhang on the sides to help remove the loaf after baking. Spray the foil with cooking spray.

In a large bowl, whisk together the flour, baking powder, salt, and sugar. Add the eggs, oil, and yogurt. Mix on medium speed with an electric mixer until well blended. Add the lemon extract and zest. Mix well.

Pour half of the cake batter into the prepared pan. Dollop half of the cream cheese mixture over the cake batter, spreading with a rubber spatula. Repeat the layers once, swirling cream cheese into the batter with a knife or toothpick.

Bake 35–40 minutes, or until the cake is golden brown and set in the center. A toothpick inserted in the center of the cake should come out with only a few crumbs. Let the loaf cool in the pan 15–20 minutes. Lift the loaf from the pan by the foil and cool completely.

To make the glaze: In a small bowl, whisk together the confectioners' sugar and lemon juice until smooth. Drizzle the glaze over the pound cake.

cornbread cake
with Maple-Bourbon Frosting

There is an age-old debate in the South when it comes to cornbread: sugar or no sugar? This cake, as you can tell, is all about the sugar. The beloved cornbread texture is altered slightly in order to produce a softer, sweeter crumb, and each layer is topped with a bourbon soak and a generous slathering of maple-bourbon frosting.

SERVES 10

For the cornbread cake:

1 ¾ cups all-purpose flour

½ cup self-rising cornmeal

1 tablespoon baking powder

½ teaspoon salt

1 ½ cups granulated sugar

¼ cup pure maple syrup

3 large eggs

½ cup vegetable or canola oil

1 teaspoon vanilla extract

1 ¼ cups whole milk

¼ cup bourbon

For the maple-bourbon frosting:

½ cup bourbon

1 cup butter, softened

1 cup vegetable shortening

2 teaspoons maple extract
   or 2 tablespoons pure
   maple syrup

6 cups confectioners' sugar

For the garnish:

Maple syrup

To make the cornbread cake: Preheat the oven to 350°F. Spray two 8-inch cake pans with cooking spray. Line the bottoms with parchment paper and spray again.

In a medium bowl, whisk together the flour, cornmeal, baking powder, and salt. Set aside. In a large bowl, combine the sugar, maple syrup, eggs, oil, and vanilla. Mix on medium speed with an electric mixer until well blended. Add half of the flour mixture and half of the milk. Mix well. Repeat with the remaining flour mixture and milk.

Divide the batter evenly between the cake pans. Bake 25–27 minutes, or until golden brown and set in the center so a toothpick inserted in center comes out clean. Let the cakes cool in the pans 10–15 minutes, then transfer to a wire rack to cool completely. Brush the bourbon over the tops of the cake layers.

To make the frosting: Heat the bourbon in a small saucepan over medium heat. Bring to a simmer. Let the bourbon cook until it reduces by half and measures ¼ cup. Remove from the heat and let cool completely.

In a large bowl, cream the butter on medium-high speed with an electric mixer. Add the shortening and mix until well blended. Add the maple extract or maple syrup, ¼ cup reduced bourbon, and half of the confectioners' sugar. Mix on low speed until mostly combined, then medium-high speed until completely combined. Repeat with the second half of the confectioners' sugar.

To assemble: Spread the frosting between the cake layers and then all over the cake. Decorate with a drizzle of maple syrup, if desired.

blackberry jam cake

This classic buttermilk cake is full of wonderful spices and blackberry jam, although it could be fun to play with the flavors and use your favorite! Traditionally topped with a caramel buttercream, I opted for a tangy blackberry cream cheese frosting.

SERVES 10

For the blackberry jam cake:

3 cups all-purpose flour

1 teaspoon baking soda

½ teaspoon ground cinnamon

¼ teaspoon ground nutmeg

¼ teaspoon allspice

¼ teaspoon salt

1½ cups granulated sugar

¼ cup packed light brown sugar

1 cup vegetable or canola oil

1 cup seedless blackberry jam

3 large eggs

1 teaspoon vanilla extract

1 cup buttermilk

1 cup chopped pecans

For the blackberry–cream cheese frosting:

½ cup butter

1 (8-ounce) package cream cheese

1 teaspoon vanilla extract

3 tablespoons seedless blackberry jam

6 cups confectioners' sugar

For the garnishes:

Fresh blackberries

Fresh flowers

Chopped pecans

To make the cake: Preheat the oven to 350°F. Grease three 8-inch cake pans with cooking spray. Line the bottom of each with parchment paper, then spray again.

In a medium bowl, whisk together the flour, baking soda, cinnamon, nutmeg, allspice, and salt. Set aside. In a large bowl, combine both sugars, oil, and blackberry jam. Mix on medium speed until well blended. Add the eggs and vanilla; mix well. Add half of the flour mixture and half of the buttermilk. Mix until the ingredients are just blended. Repeat with the second half of the flour and buttermilk. Mix until the batter is smooth. Fold in the pecans.

Divide the batter evenly among the cake pans and bake 23–25 minutes, or until the cake layers are golden brown on top and a toothpick inserted into the center comes out clean. Let the cake layers cool in the pans 5–10 minutes, then transfer to a wire rack to cool completely.

To make frosting: In a large bowl, cream the butter and cream cheese with an electric mixer on medium-high speed until smooth. Add the vanilla, jam, and half of the confectioners' sugar. Mix on low speed until mostly combined, then medium-high speed until completely combined. Repeat with the second half of the confectioners' sugar.

To assemble the cake: Place a cake layer on a cake plate or stand. Spread with the frosting. Repeat with the second two layers, and then spread the frosting around the entire cake. Garnish with fresh blackberries, fresh flowers, and pecans, if desired.

bourbon–vanilla bean caramel cake

My homage to the classic Southern caramel cake—a moist, buttery cake topped with a boozy caramel sauce.

SERVES 10

For the bourbon–vanilla bean caramel sauce:

1 cup granulated sugar

6 tablespoons cold butter, diced

¼ cup heavy whipping cream

1 tablespoon vanilla bean paste

3 tablespoons bourbon

Pinch of salt

For the butter cake:

3 cups all-purpose flour

1 tablespoon baking powder

½ teaspoon baking soda

½ teaspoon salt

1 cup butter, room temperature

2 cups granulated sugar

1 tablespoon vanilla bean paste (or vanilla extract)

4 large eggs

¼ cup vegetable or canola oil

1½ cups buttermilk

To make the caramel sauce: Place the sugar in a medium-size saucepan over medium heat. Stir occasionally until the sugar begins to clump together. Continue cooking until the clumps begin to melt and turn an amber color. Stir occasionally until completely melted. While stirring, add the cubed butter gradually until melted. Gradually add the cream until incorporated. Reduce the heat to low and continue cooking for an additional minute. Remove from the heat and stir in the vanilla, bourbon, and salt. Let cool completely before using.

To make the cake: Preheat the oven to 350°F. Grease three 8-inch cake pans with cooking spray. Line the pans with parchment paper, and spray again.

In a medium bowl, whisk together the flour, baking powder, baking soda, and salt. Set aside.

In a large bowl, cream the butter on medium-high speed until smooth. Add the sugar and vanilla bean paste; mix until fluffy. Add the eggs and oil; mix until well blended. Add half of the flour mixture and half of the buttermilk. Mix until mostly combined. Add the remaining flour and buttermilk; mix until incorporated.

Divide the batter evenly among the prepared pans. Bake 25–27 minutes, or until golden brown and a toothpick inserted into the center comes out clean. Let the cake layers cool in the pans for 10–15 minutes, then transfer to a wire rack to cool completely.

To make the frosting: In a large bowl, cream the butter and shortening together on medium-high speed until smooth. Add the vanilla and caramel sauce, and mix well. Add half of the confectioners' sugar and mix until incorporated. Repeat with the second half of the confectioners' sugar.

For the caramel frosting:

1 cup butter, room
    temperature

1 cup vegetable shortening

1 teaspoon vanilla extract

3 tablespoons salted caramel
    sauce

5 cups confectioners' sugar

For the garnish:

Caramel corn

To assemble the cake: Place one cake layer on a plate or cake stand. Spread the top with a thin layer of frosting. Repeat with the next two layers, then cover the whole cake with frosting. Next, pour about ½ cup prepared caramel sauce onto the center of the frosted cake. (If the caramel sauce is too thick, try warming it up slightly and stirring well.) Spread the sauce outward toward the edges of the cake with a rubber or offset spatula. Gradually add more caramel sauce as needed, and let it roll down the edges. Let the caramel sauce set for a few minutes before decorating with caramel corn.

death by chocolate mousse cake

Reminiscent of potlucks and family lunches, this Death by Chocolate Mousse Cake is a dressed-up version of the traditional pudding-like dessert, but you'll still get a taste of rich chocolate cake, luxurious mousse, and fluffy whipped cream in every bite!

SERVES 8–10

For the chocolate cake:

¾ cup all-purpose flour

¼ cup cocoa powder

1 teaspoon baking powder

1 teaspoon baking soda

½ teaspoon salt

1 large egg

⅔ cup granulated sugar

⅓ cup vegetable or canola oil

1 teaspoon vanilla extract

⅔ cup whole milk

For the chocolate mousse:

1 (4-ounce) semisweet chocolate bar, chopped

1 tablespoon coconut oil

2 large egg whites

½ cup granulated sugar

¼ teaspoon cream of tartar

1 cup heavy whipping cream

For the whipped cream:

1½ cups heavy whipping cream

2 tablespoons confectioners' sugar

1 teaspoon vanilla extract

For the garnish:

Chocolate chips

Chopped pecans

To make the cake: Preheat the oven to 350°F. Spray a 9-inch springform pan with cooking spray. Set the pan on a sheet of aluminum foil, and wrap up the sides of the pan to prevent leaks while baking.

Whisk together the flour, cocoa powder, baking powder, baking soda, and salt in a medium bowl. Set aside. In a large bowl, combine the egg, sugar, oil, and vanilla. Mix on medium speed with an electric mixer until well blended. Add the flour mixture and milk; mix until combined.

Pour the batter into the prepared pan and bake 25–27 minutes, or until the center is set and a toothpick inserted into the center comes out clean. Let the cake cool completely.

To make the mousse: Place the chocolate and coconut oil in a small heat-safe dish and microwave in 30-second intervals, stirring between each, until melted and smooth. Set aside. Place the egg whites, sugar, and cream of tartar in a medium heat-safe bowl. Boil 2 inches of water in a medium saucepan and set the bowl on top (or use a double boiler). Make sure the bottom of the bowl does not touch the boiling water. Whisk continuously until the sugar has dissolved, about 4 minutes. Remove from the heat. Whip the egg white mixture on high speed with an electric mixer until glossy and stiff peaks form. Gently fold the melted chocolate into the meringue. Whip the heavy cream on high speed with an electric mixer until stiff peaks form. Fold the whipped cream into the meringue mixture. Spread the mousse on top of the chocolate cake in the springform pan.

To make the whipped cream: In the bowl of a stand mixer using the whisk attachment, whip the heavy cream, confectioners' sugar, and vanilla on high speed until stiff peaks form.

To assemble the cake: Spread the whipped cream over the mousse and sprinkle with chocolate chips and chopped pecans. Store loosely covered in the refrigerator. Remove from the springform pan to slice and serve.

texas sheet cake
with Brown Sugar Bacon

You can't go wrong with chocolate sheet cake when feeding a large group. Add a sprinkle of sweet and salty bacon and you're sure to have everyone's new favorite!

SERVES 18–20

For the brown sugar bacon:

⅓ cup loosely packed light brown sugar

4 strips thick-cut bacon

For the Texas sheet cake:

1 cup butter

¼ cup unsweetened cocoa powder

1 cup water

2 cups granulated sugar

2 cups all-purpose flour

Pinch of ground cinnamon

½ teaspoon salt

½ cup buttermilk

1 teaspoon vanilla extract

3 large eggs

1 teaspoon baking soda

For the fudge frosting:

1 cup butter

¼ cup unsweetened cocoa powder

½ cup whole milk

1 teaspoon vanilla extract

1 (1-pound) package confectioners' sugar

½ cup chopped pecans, toasted

To make the brown sugar bacon: Preheat the oven to 400°F. Line a baking sheet with aluminum foil. Spread the brown sugar in a small shallow dish. Dredge both sides of the bacon strips in sugar, and lay them on the baking sheet. Bake 14–16 minutes, or until the bacon is crisp. Let the bacon cool completely, and chop it into small pieces.

To make the cake: Preheat the oven to 350°F. Spray a 9 × 13-inch pan with cooking spray. Melt the butter in a medium-size saucepan over medium heat. Add the cocoa powder and water. Bring to a boil, then remove from the heat. In a large bowl, whisk together the sugar, flour, cinnamon, and salt. Add the chocolate mixture, whisking to combine. Stir together the buttermilk, vanilla, eggs, and baking soda in a small bowl. Add to the cake batter, and whisk until well blended. Pour the cake batter into the prepared pan and bake for 20 minutes, or until set in the center.

To make the fudge frosting: (You can use the same saucepan as before.) Melt the butter in a medium-size saucepan over medium heat. Add the cocoa powder, and bring the mixture to a simmer. Cook for 20 seconds, then remove from the heat. Stir in the milk and vanilla. Add the confectioners' sugar, and whisk until smooth.

To assemble the cake: Pour the frosting over the warm cake, and spread evenly with a spoon or rubber spatula. Immediately sprinkle with pecans and chopped bacon. Let the frosting set before slicing and serving.

peanut butter lover's cake

If you dream in layers of peanut butter and fluffy peanut butter clouds, this cake is for you! The real star of this cake, the peanut butter ganache, can be prepared in advance but is best used directly after it's made.

SERVES 10

For the peanut butter ganache:

1 cup peanut butter chips

⅔ cup heavy whipping cream

For the peanut butter cake:

2¼ cups all-purpose flour

1 teaspoon baking soda

1 teaspoon baking powder

½ teaspoon salt

1 cup butter, softened

½ cup creamy peanut butter

1½ cups granulated sugar

¼ cup packed light brown sugar

1 teaspoon vanilla extract

3 large eggs

1¼ cups buttermilk

For the peanut butter frosting:

1 cup butter, softened

½ cup vegetable shortening

½ cup creamy peanut butter

1 teaspoon vanilla extract

2 tablespoons whole milk

5 cups confectioners' sugar

For the garnish:

Chopped peanuts

To make the peanut butter ganache: Place the peanut butter chips and cream in a small saucepan over medium-low heat. Stir continuously until melted and smooth. Set aside to cool completely.

To make the cake: Preheat the oven to 350°F. Spray four 6-inch (or three 8-inch) cake pans with cooking spray.

Whisk together the flour, baking soda, baking powder, and salt. Set aside. In a large bowl, cream the butter on medium-high speed with an electric mixer until smooth. Add the peanut butter, and mix until well blended with the butter. Add both sugars and vanilla. Mix until fluffy. Add the eggs and mix well. Add half of the flour mixture and half of the buttermilk; mix until just combined. Repeat with the second half of the flour mixture and the buttermilk until incorporated.

Divide the batter evenly among the cake pans and bake 23–25 minutes, or until the cakes are golden brown and a toothpick inserted into the center of each cake layer comes out with only a few crumbs. Let the cakes cool in their pans 10–15 minutes, then transfer to a wire rack to cool completely.

To make the frosting: In a large bowl, cream the butter and shortening on medium-high speed with an electric mixer until smooth. Add the peanut butter, vanilla, and milk. Mix well. Add half of the confectioners' sugar, mixing until combined. Repeat with the second half of the confectioners' sugar.

To assemble: Place a cake layer on a cake plate or stand. Spread with peanut butter frosting. Repeat with the remaining cake layers, and then spread frosting over the outside of the cake. Using a squeeze bottle or a piping bag with a small tip cut off, drip the ganache onto the top edge of the cake, and let it roll over and down the sides. Then pipe ganache onto the center of the cake and spread (with a rubber or offset spatula) to the edges of the cake. Garnish with any remaining frosting and chopped peanuts.

raspberry-peach coffee cake

I'm of the opinion that even brunch can have dessert. The best part of this cake is when you get a bit of fruit, streusel, and glaze all in one bite! It's the kind of cake that keeps you sneaking into the kitchen to cut a small slice.

SERVES 8

For the streusel:

1 cup all-purpose flour

¼ cup packed light brown sugar, packed

¼ cup granulated sugar

1 teaspoon ground cinnamon

Pinch of salt

½ cup cold butter, cubed

For the cake:

1¾ cups all-purpose flour

2 teaspoons baking powder

½ teaspoon salt

½ cup vegetable or canola oil

1 cup granulated sugar

2 large eggs

1 teaspoon almond extract (or use vanilla extract)

¾ cup whole milk

1 cup fresh raspberries

1 cup peeled and diced fresh peaches

For the glaze:

1 cup confectioners' sugar

½ teaspoon almond extract

3–4 tablespoons whole milk

To make the streusel: In a medium bowl, whisk together all streusel ingredients except the butter. Cut the butter into the flour mixture with a pastry cutter (or two knives, or your hands) until the texture resembles wet sand. Set aside.

To make the cake: Preheat the oven to 350°F. Spray a 9-inch spring-form pan with cooking spray. Set the springform pan on a sheet of aluminum foil, and fold the edges up the sides to prevent leaking.

In a large bowl, combine the flour, baking powder, salt, oil, sugar, eggs, almond extract, and milk. Mix on medium speed with an electric mixer until the ingredients are incorporated and the batter is smooth. Pour the batter into the prepared pan. Arrange the raspberries and peaches over the top. Sprinkle evenly with streusel.

Bake 40–45 minutes, or until the streusel is golden brown and the cake is set in the center. Remove from the oven, and run a knife around the inside edge of the pan to loosen the cake. Let the cake cool 15–20 minutes before removing the springform pan.

To make the glaze: While the cake is cooling, in a medium bowl, whisk together the confectioners' sugar, almond extract, and milk until smooth. Drizzle the glaze over the streusel.

caramel apple upside-down cake

Caramel and apple is one of my all-time favorite flavor combinations. They just pair so well together in almost every kind of dessert, and the combination never fails to remind me of autumn. Enjoy this upside-down cake as a morning or afternoon snack!

SERVES 8

For the caramel sauce:

½ cup granulated sugar

¼ cup cold butter, cubed

¼ cup water

½ teaspoon salt

¼ teaspoon ground cinnamon

For the cake:

2 medium apples, peeled and thinly sliced

1¼ cups all-purpose flour

1 teaspoon baking powder

½ teaspoon ground cinnamon

¼ teaspoon ground nutmeg

½ teaspoon salt

1 cup granulated sugar

¼ cup packed light brown sugar

½ cup vegetable oil

2 large eggs

1 teaspoon vanilla extract

½ cup whole milk

¼ cup caramel sauce

To make the caramel sauce: Heat the sugar in a small saucepan over medium-high heat until it begins to melt on the bottom. Stir occasionally until the sugar forms clumps. Let the sugar continue to cook, stirring frequently, until it is melted and amber in color. Add the butter a few pieces at a time, stirring continuously. The mixture will bubble up. Continue stirring, slowly drizzling in the water. Reduce the heat to medium-low and let the caramel cook, without stirring, for 1 minute. Remove from the heat. Stir in the salt and cinnamon.

To make the cake: Preheat the oven to 350°F. Spray a 9-inch cake pan with cooking spray. Line the pan with a circle of parchment paper, and spray again. Arrange the sliced apples over the bottom of the pan.

In a large bowl, combine all of the cake ingredients except the caramel. Mix on medium speed with an electric mixer until the batter is smooth. Add the ¼ cup caramel, and mix until incorporated.

Pour the remaining caramel sauce over the apples in the pan. Pour the batter over the apples and caramel. Bake 30–35 minutes, or until set in the center and golden brown. Remove from the oven, and run a knife around the edges of the cake to loosen it from the pan. Let the cake cool 5–10 minutes before inverting it onto a cake plate. Discard the parchment paper. This cake is best served warm.

praline banana bread

Banana bread is one of those recipes that is easily dressed up—fill it with nuts and chocolate chips or a thick cinnamon swirl, top it with a crumble or a nice glaze. But I am here to tell you that you should be serving it with praline sauce, so now you know!

SERVES 8

For the banana bread:

2 large, very ripe bananas, mashed

⅓ cup vegetable oil

¼ cup plain Greek yogurt

½ cup granulated sugar

¼ cup packed light brown sugar

2 large eggs

1 teaspoon vanilla extract

1½ cups all-purpose flour

1 teaspoon baking soda

½ teaspoon salt

½ teaspoon ground cinnamon

½ cup chopped pecans

For the praline sauce:

4 tablespoons butter

½ cup packed dark brown sugar

2 tablespoons heavy whipping cream (or whole milk)

½ teaspoon vanilla extract

Pinch of salt

¼ cup chopped pecans

To make the bread: Preheat the oven to 350°F. Grease an 8 X 4-inch loaf pan with cooking spray.

In a large bowl, combine all of the banana bread ingredients, except the pecans, and mix on medium speed with an electric mixer until smooth. Fold in the pecans. Pour the batter into the prepared pan, and bake 40–45 minutes, or until a toothpick inserted into the center of the loaf comes out with only a few crumbs. Remove the loaf from the oven and let cool 10–15 minutes. Transfer to a wire rack to cool completely.

To make the praline sauce: Melt the butter in a medium saucepan over medium heat. Add the dark brown sugar, and whisk continuously until it melts and the mixture begins to boil, about 5 minutes. Stir in the cream, vanilla, salt, and pecans. Drizzle the praline sauce over the banana bread.

pineapple upside-down bundt cake

This isn't your grandma's pineapple upside-down cake. Impress your friends and family by arranging pineapple slices and cherries along the bottom of a Bundt cake pan!

SERVES 12

For the topping:

½ cup butter, melted

½ cup packed light brown sugar

1 (20-ounce) can pineapple rings in juice, drained (juice reserved)

1 (10-ounce) jar stemless maraschino cherries

For the cake:

2 cups all-purpose flour

1 tablespoon baking powder

½ teaspoon salt

1½ cups granulated sugar

3 large eggs

½ cup canola oil

1 teaspoon vanilla extract

¼ cup reserved pineapple juice

½ cup whole milk

To make the topping: Preheat the oven to 350°F. Spray a Bundt cake pan with cooking spray. Pour the melted butter into the bottom of the pan. Sprinkle evenly with the brown sugar. Cut the pineapple rings in half, and arrange them in the grooves of the Bundt cake pan. Arrange the cherries between the pineapple rings.

To make the cake: In a medium bowl, whisk together the flour, baking powder, and salt. Set aside. In a large bowl, combine the sugar, eggs, oil, and vanilla. Mix on medium speed with an electric mixer until just blended. Add the flour mixture, pineapple juice, and milk to the wet ingredients. Mix until well blended.

Carefully spoon the batter over the pineapple and cherries in the Bundt pan. Bake 40–45 minutes, or until the cake is set in the middle and a toothpick inserted into the center comes out clean. Let the cake cool in the pan 5–10 minutes, then turn it out onto a wire rack or cake plate to cool completely.

campfire cake

Alternate layers of chocolate and graham cracker cake are secretly filled with homemade marshmallow, and the entire cake is covered in a rich chocolate buttercream. This cake will have s'mores lovers dreaming of summer camping trips and bonfires!

SERVES 10

For the chocolate cake:

1¾ cups all-purpose flour

¾ cup unsweetened cocoa powder

1¼ teaspoons baking soda

½ teaspoon baking powder

½ teaspoon salt

2 cups granulated sugar

2 large eggs

½ cup vegetable oil

1 teaspoon vanilla extract

1 cup whole milk

For the graham cracker cake:

1½ cups all-purpose flour

1 cup graham cracker crumbs

1 tablespoon baking powder

½ teaspoon salt

1½ cups granulated sugar

3 large eggs

½ cup vegetable oil

1 teaspoon vanilla extract

1 cup whole milk

To make the chocolate cake: Preheat the oven to 350°F. Spray two 8-inch cake pans with cooking spray. Line the pans with parchment paper and spray again. In a medium bowl, whisk together the flour, cocoa powder, baking soda, baking powder, and salt. In a large bowl, combine the sugar, eggs, oil, and vanilla. Mix on medium speed with an electric mixer until smooth. Add the flour mixture and milk. Mix until well blended. Divide the batter evenly between the cake pans, and bake 30–35 minutes, or until the center is set and a toothpick inserted into the center comes out clean. Let the cakes cool in the pans 10–15 minutes, then transfer to a wire rack to cool completely.

To make the graham cracker cake: Preheat the oven to 350°F. Spray two 8-inch cake pans with cooking spray. Line the pans with parchment paper and spray again. Whisk together the flour, graham cracker crumbs, baking powder, and salt in a medium bowl. In a large bowl, combine the sugar, eggs, oil, and vanilla. Mix on medium speed with an electric mixer until smooth. Add the flour mixture and milk. Mix until well blended. Divide the batter evenly between cake pans, and bake 25–30 minutes, or until the center is set and a toothpick inserted into the center comes out clean. Let the cakes cool in the pans 10–15 minutes, then transfer to a wire rack to cool completely.

To make the marshmallow filling: Combine the corn syrup and sugar in a small saucepan over medium-high heat. Clip a candy thermometer to the side of the pan, and bring the mixture to a simmer. While the syrup mixture is heating, combine the egg whites and cream of tartar in the bowl of a stand mixer fitted with the whisk attachment. Whip the egg whites until soft peaks form. When the candy thermometer reaches 240°F, remove from the heat. With the mixer running, carefully pour the syrup in a steady stream into the egg whites. Continue whipping until the mixture is thick, glossy, and stiff peaks form. Mix in the vanilla.

For the marshmallow filling:

¾ cup light corn syrup

1 cup granulated sugar

3 large egg whites

½ teaspoon cream of tartar

1 teaspoon vanilla extract

For the chocolate frosting:

1 cup butter, softened

⅓ cup unsweetened cocoa powder

1 teaspoon vanilla extract

4 cups confectioners' sugar

1–2 tablespoons whole milk

For the garnishes:

Any remaining Marshmallow Filling

Chocolate sauce or ganache

Graham crackers or crumbs

Chopped chocolate

To assemble the cake: On a cake stand or cake plate, place one chocolate cake layer, and spread it with marshmallow filling. Repeat with a graham cracker cake layer and the second chocolate cake layer. Place the final graham cracker cake layer on top. Transfer the cake to the refrigerator for 20–30 minutes. (I find it easier to frost a cold cake.)

To make the chocolate frosting: In a large bowl, cream the butter on medium-high speed with an electric mixer until smooth. Add the cocoa powder and vanilla. Add half of the confectioners' sugar; mix until well blended. Add the second half of the confectioners' sugar and all of the milk; mix until incorporated and the frosting is fluffy.

To finish: Remove the cake from the refrigerator, and cover the outside with chocolate frosting. Pipe any remaining marshmallow frosting around the top edges of the cake. Garnish with chocolate sauce, graham crackers, and chopped chocolate.

blueberry-almond buckle

I'm all about treating yourself with cake for breakfast if the occasion arises! This buckle is dotted with fresh blueberries, crunchy topping, and a sweet almond glaze.

SERVES 9

For the topping:

1 cup packed light brown sugar

¾ cup all-purpose flour

½ cup finely chopped almonds

½ teaspoon cinnamon

½ cup cold butter, diced

For the blueberry cake:

½ cup butter, softened

¾ cup granulated sugar

¼ cup plain Greek yogurt

1 large egg

1 teaspoon almond extract

½ cup buttermilk

2 cups all-purpose flour

2 teaspoons baking powder

½ teaspoon salt

2 cups fresh blueberries

For the almond glaze:

1 cup confectioners' sugar

1 teaspoon almond extract

2 tablespoons whole milk

For the garnish:

Sliced almonds (optional)

To make the crumb topping: Combine all the ingredients in a medium bowl. Using a pastry cutter (or two knives or two forks), cut the butter into the dry ingredients until a crumbly mixture forms. Set aside.

To make the cake: Preheat the oven to 350°F. Spray a 9-inch square baking dish with cooking spray. In a large bowl, cream the butter on medium-high speed with an electric mixer. Add the sugar and mix until fluffy. Add the yogurt, egg, almond extract, and buttermilk; mix well. Add the flour, baking powder, and salt. Mix until well blended. Fold in the blueberries. Pour the batter into the pan, and spread with a rubber spatula. Sprinkle evenly with crumb topping. Bake 35–40 minutes, or until a toothpick inserted into the center of the cake comes out clean. Let the cake cool completely.

To make the glaze: Whisk together the confectioners' sugar, almond extract, and milk until smooth. Drizzle over the cake. Sprinkle with sliced almonds, if desired.

sweet potato–cornbread cupcakes
with Cinnamon-Honey Buttercream

These cupcakes were inspired by—waffles? That's right! I ordered sweet potato cornbread waffles at a restaurant in Charleston a couple of years ago and have been wanting to riff off them ever since. They were served with whipped cinnamon honey butter and maple syrup.

MAKES 24

For the sweet potato cornbread cupcakes:

1¼ cups all-purpose flour

1 cup yellow cornmeal

1 tablespoon baking powder

½ teaspoon cinnamon

½ teaspoon salt

¾ cup mashed cooked (cooled) sweet potato

1 cup granulated sugar

½ cup packed light brown sugar

3 large eggs

1 teaspoon vanilla extract

½ cup vegetable oil

1 cup whole milk

For the cinnamon-honey buttercream:

1 cup butter, softened

1 cup vegetable shortening

½ teaspoon cinnamon

3 tablespoons honey

6 cups confectioners' sugar

For the garnishes:

Pecan halves

Honey

Caramel sauce

To make the cupcakes: Preheat the oven to 350°F. Line two 12-cup muffin pans with paper liners. In a medium bowl, whisk together the flour, cornmeal, baking powder, cinnamon, and salt. Set aside. In a large bowl, combine the sweet potato, both sugars, eggs, vanilla, and oil. Mix on medium speed with an electric mixer until smooth. Add the flour mixture and milk. Mix until all ingredients are incorporated. Using a cookie scoop, scoop the batter into the paper liners until about two-thirds full. Bake 20–22 minutes, or until lightly browned on the top. Remove from the oven and let cool completely.

To make the frosting: In a large bowl, beat the butter on medium-high speed with an electric mixer until smooth and creamy. Add the shortening and mix well. Add the cinnamon, honey, and half of the confectioners' sugar. Mix on low speed until the ingredients are mostly combined, then on medium-high speed until well blended. Repeat with the second half of the confectioners' sugar.

To assemble the cupcakes: Use a piping bag or spread the frosting on top of each cupcake. Top with pecan halves and drizzle with honey and caramel sauce.

alabama lane cake

If you've read To Kill a Mockingbird, *maybe you'll remember a reference to Alabama Lane Cake. The cake is moist and fluffy, but it's most well known for the filling, which is flavored with bourbon, pecans, coconut, and dried fruit.*

SERVES 24

For the cake:

1½ cups granulated sugar

1 cup vegetable oil

2 teaspoons vanilla extract

3 cups all-purpose flour

1 tablespoon baking powder

½ teaspoon salt

1¼ cups whole milk

7 large egg whites (yolks reserved for filling)

For the filling:

7 large egg yolks, beaten

1 cup granulated sugar

½ cup butter

1 cup chopped pecans

1 cup shredded coconut

1 cup diced dried cherries (or raisins)

1 teaspoon vanilla extract

⅓ cup bourbon

For the vanilla buttercream:

1 cup butter, softened

½ cup vegetable shortening

1 tablespoon vanilla extract

5 cups confectioners' sugar

For the garnish:

Maraschino cherries

To make the cake: Preheat the oven to 350°F. Spray three 8-inch cake pans with cooking spray. Combine the sugar, oil, and vanilla in a large bowl. Mix on medium speed until blended. Add the flour, baking powder, salt, and milk. Mix until well blended. In a separate bowl, beat the egg whites on high speed until stiff peaks form. Fold into the cake batter. Divide the batter evenly among the prepared pans, and bake 25–28 minutes, or until lightly golden brown on top and a toothpick inserted into the center comes out clean. Let the cakes cool in the pans for 10–15 minutes, then transfer to a wire rack to cool completely.

To make the filling: Combine the egg yolks, sugar, and butter in a medium saucepan over medium-low heat. Cook, stirring constantly, until the mixture thickens enough to coat the back of a spoon. Stir in the pecans, coconut, cherries, vanilla, and bourbon. Continue stirring 2–3 minutes, then remove from the heat, and let the filling cool completely.

To make the frosting: In a large bowl, cream the butter and shortening on medium-high speed with an electric mixer until smooth. Add the vanilla and half of the confectioners' sugar; mix until well blended. Repeat with the second half of the confectioners' sugar. Mix an additional minute until fluffy and smooth.

To assemble cake: Place one cake layer on a plate or cake stand. Pipe a ring of frosting around the top of the cake layer; fill with the filling. Repeat with the second cake layer, frosting, and filling. Top with the third cake layer. Spread the frosting around the outside of the cake. Garnish with cherries and filling, if desired.

lemon poppy-seed cake

This cake is a go-to when you need something simple and classic. With the moist crumb and silky frosting, it's bright and flavorful and has a little bit of sunshine in every bite.

SERVES 10

For the cake:

2¼ cups all-purpose flour

1 tablespoon baking powder

½ teaspoon salt

2 tablespoons poppy seeds

1½ cups granulated sugar

½ cup canola oil

3 large eggs

1 teaspoon lemon extract

1 tablespoon lemon zest

¼ cup fresh lemon juice

1 cup whole milk

For the lemon–cream cheese frosting:

1 (8-ounce) package cream cheese, softened

½ cup butter, softened

1 teaspoon lemon extract

½ tablespoon lemon zest

6 cups confectioners' sugar

For the garnishes:

Lemon slices

Lemon zest

Flowers

To make the cake: Preheat the oven to 350°F. Spray two 8-inch cake pans with nonstick spray. Line the pans with parchment paper and spray again. In a medium bowl, whisk together the flour, baking powder, salt, and poppy seeds. Set aside. In a large bowl, combine the sugar, oil, eggs, lemon extract, zest, and lemon juice. Mix on medium speed with an electric mixer until smooth. Add half of the flour mixture and half of the milk. Mix until just blended. Repeat with the remaining flour and milk.

Divide the batter evenly between cake pans, and bake 22–25 minutes, or until golden and a toothpick inserted into the center comes out clean. Let the cakes cool in the pans for 5 minutes, then transfer to a wire rack to cool completely.

To make the frosting: In a large bowl, beat the cream cheese and butter on medium speed with an electric mixer until smooth. Add the lemon extract, zest, and half of the confectioners' sugar. Mix until smooth. Repeat with the remaining confectioners' sugar, mixing for an additional minute, until smooth and fluffy.

To assemble cake: Place one cake layer on a plate or cake stand. Spread with the frosting. Place the second cake layer on top, and spread the frosting over the outside of the cake. Garnish with lemons and flowers as desired.

strawberries and cream sheet cake

There's nothing better than an old-fashioned strawberry cake! This cake gets some extra flavor from pulverized freeze-dried berries. Feel free to chop up some fresh strawberries to stir into the cake batter!

SERVES 24

For the cake:

1 (1-ounce) package freeze-dried strawberries

½ (3-ounce) package strawberry gelatin

2 cups all-purpose flour

1 tablespoon baking powder

½ teaspoon salt

1½ cups granulated sugar

3 large eggs

½ cup vegetable oil (or canola oil)

1 tablespoon vanilla extract

1¼ cups whole milk

For the vanilla bean buttercream:

1 cup butter, softened

½ cup vegetable shortening

1 vanilla bean, split and seeds reserved

1 teaspoon vanilla extract

5 cups confectioners' sugar

For the garnish

Strawberries

To make the cake: Preheat the oven to 350°F. Spray a 9 X 13-inch pan with cooking spray. Line with parchment paper and spray again.

Place the freeze-dried strawberries in a food processor, and process until the texture resembles fine powder. Whisk together the processed strawberries, gelatin, flour, baking powder, and salt in a medium bowl. In a large bowl, combine the sugar, eggs, oil, and vanilla. Mix on medium speed with an electric mixer until well blended. Add the flour mixture and milk; mix until combined. Pour the batter into the prepared cake pan, and bake 25–28 minutes, or until a toothpick inserted into the center of the cake comes out clean. Let the cake cool completely before frosting.

To make the frosting: In a large bowl, beat the butter and shortening on medium speed with an electric mixer until smooth. Add the vanilla bean seeds, vanilla extract, and half of the confectioners' sugar. Mix until well blended. Add the second half of the confectioners' sugar, and mix for an additional minute, until combined and fluffy.

To assemble the cake: Spread the frosting over the cooled cake. Garnish with strawberries.

coconut rum pineapple shortcakes

Layer up some boozy pineapple and fluffy coconut whipped cream with these buttery coconut shortcakes for a fresh, summery twist on traditional strawberry shortcakes! These from-scratch biscuits have coconut right in the dough.

MAKES 8

For the pineapple:

1 fresh pineapple, peeled and sliced, core discarded (or use canned)

¾ cup coconut rum

½ cup packed light brown sugar

For the coconut biscuits:

2 cups all-purpose flour

2 teaspoons baking powder

¼ cup granulated sugar

Pinch of salt

½ cup cold butter, cubed

1 teaspoon coconut extract

½ cup buttermilk

½ cup shredded coconut

2 tablespoons butter, melted

For the coconut whipped cream:

2 cups heavy whipping cream

3 tablespoons confectioners' sugar

1 teaspoon coconut extract

To soak the pineapple: Lay the pineapple slices in a 9 X 13-inch baking pan. Stir together the coconut rum and brown sugar; pour over the pineapple. Transfer the pan to the fridge, and let the pineapple soak for 30 minutes to 1 hour.

After the pineapple has soaked, pour the marinade into a small saucepan over medium heat. Bring the mixture to a simmer, and cook, stirring occasionally, until thickened and syrupy. Remove from the heat and allow to cool.

To make the biscuits: Preheat the oven to 425°F. Line a baking sheet with parchment paper. Whisk together the flour, baking powder, sugar, and salt in a large bowl. Use a pastry blender to cut the butter into the dry ingredients until the mixture is crumbly. Add the coconut extract and buttermilk; stir until mostly combined. Fold in the shredded coconut. Using a cookie scoop, drop batter into 8 equal portions on the parchment paper. Brush with melted butter. Bake 12–15 minutes, or until golden brown. Remove from the oven and cool completely.

To make the whipped cream: In the bowl of a stand mixer using the whisk attachment, beat the cream, confectioners' sugar, and coconut extract on high until stiff peaks form.

To assemble the shortcakes: Split the biscuits, and layer them with the rum-soaked pineapple and whipped cream. Serve with the rum sauce.

cheesecakes

frozen coconut–key lime cheesecake

Frozen cheesecakes are perfect for those hot Southern days when you don't want to turn on your oven and heat up your kitchen. You don't even need to bake the crust! Just whip up the fillings, spread into a springform pan, and pop it in the freezer for a sweet, frozen treat.

SERVES 10

For the crust:

1½ cups graham cracker crumbs

6 tablespoons butter, melted

For the coconut layer:

1 (8-ounce) package cream cheese, softened

1 (6-ounce) container coconut Greek yogurt

½ cup confectioners' sugar

1 teaspoon coconut extract

⅓ cup flaked sweetened coconut

2 cups heavy whipping cream

For the Key lime layer:

1 (8-ounce) package cream cheese, softened

1 (6-ounce) container plain Greek yogurt

1¼ cups confectioners' sugar

¼ cup bottled Key lime juice

1 tablespoon lime zest

For the garnishes:

Whipped cream

Lime zest

Lime slices

Shredded coconut

To make the crust: Combine the graham cracker crumbs and butter; stir until the crumbs are evenly coated. Press into the bottom of a 9-inch springform pan.

To make the coconut layer: In a medium bowl, beat the cream cheese on medium speed with an electric mixer until smooth. Add the yogurt, confectioners' sugar, and coconut extract; mix well. Fold in the flaked coconut. In the large bowl of a stand mixer using the whisk attachment, beat the heavy cream on high speed until stiff peaks form. Fold half of the whipped cream into the coconut mixture, reserving the other half for the Key lime layer. Spread the coconut cheesecake filling over the crust. Transfer the pan to the freezer.

To make the Key lime layer: Beat the cream cheese on medium speed with an electric mixer until smooth. Add the yogurt, confectioners' sugar, Key lime juice, and lime zest; mix until all ingredients are incorporated. Fold in remaining half of the whipped cream. Spread the Key lime filling over the coconut filling in the pan. Return to the freezer, and chill for 4–6 hours.

To serve: Let the cheesecake thaw for 5–10 minutes before serving. Garnish with additional whipped cream, zest, lime slices, and flaked coconut, if desired.

chocolate whiskey cheesecake
with Pretzel Crust

This is the dessert you should make when you're craving something rich and decadent. The salty pretzel crust perfectly balances the sweetness, and there's even whiskey in the whipped cream!

SERVES 12

For the pretzel crust:

2 cups pretzel crumbs (about 6 cups of mini pretzels, processed)

½ cup butter, melted

For the chocolate whiskey cheesecake:

3 (8-ounce) packages cream cheese, room temperature

1 (6-ounce) container plain Greek yogurt

¾ cup granulated sugar

⅓ cup unsweetened cocoa powder

1 teaspoon vanilla extract

½ teaspoon salt

4 ounces milk chocolate, melted and cooled

⅓ cup whiskey

For the whiskey whipped cream:

1 cup heavy whipping cream

2 tablespoons confectioners' sugar

3 tablespoons whiskey

To make the crust: Preheat the oven to 350°F. Lightly grease a 9-inch springform pan. Combine the crumbs and butter, stirring until all crumbs are coated. Press the crust mixture into the bottom and slightly up the sides of the springform pan. Set aside.

To make the cheesecake: In a large bowl, beat the cream cheese on medium speed with an electric mixer until smooth. Add the yogurt, sugar, cocoa powder, vanilla, and salt; mix well. Add the chocolate and whiskey, and mix until completely incorporated. Pour the cheesecake batter over the crust in the pan. Bake for 1 hour, or until the edges of the cheesecake are set and the center is still slightly jiggly. Turn off the oven and crack the oven door; let the cheesecake sit in the oven until the oven is cool. (This helps prevent cracks in your cheesecake.)

Remove the cheesecake from the oven and let it cool to room temperature. Cover and chill in the refrigerator for 4–6 hours, or overnight.

To make the whipped cream: In the bowl of a stand mixer using the whisk attachment, combine the cream, confectioners' sugar, and whiskey. Whip on medium-high speed until stiff peaks form. Spread the whipped cream over the chilled cheesecake. Store covered in the refrigerator or cut into slices to serve.

cinnamon roll cheesecake

When I first made this cheesecake a couple of years ago, I decided to throw some Greek yogurt in the filling and discovered that it adds an extra level of creaminess. Now I always include yogurt in my cheesecakes!

SERVES 10

For the crust:

1½ cups cinnamon graham cracker crumbs

½ cup butter, melted

For the cheesecake filling:

3 (8-ounce) packages cream cheese, softened

1 (6-ounce) container vanilla Greek yogurt

¾ cup granulated sugar

1 teaspoon vanilla extract

½ teaspoon cinnamon

4 large eggs

⅓ cup cinnamon chips

For the cinnamon swirl:

3 tablespoons butter, melted

4 tablespoons packed light brown sugar

2 teaspoons cinnamon

To make the crust: Preheat the oven to 350°F. Spray a 9-inch springform pan with nonstick spray. Wrap aluminum foil around the bottom and up the sides of the pan to prevent leaking. In a small bowl, stir together the graham cracker crumbs and butter. Press the crust mixture into the bottom of the prepared pan.

To make the filling: In a large bowl, beat the cream cheese with an electric mixer on medium speed until smooth. Add the yogurt, sugar, vanilla, and cinnamon; mix well. Add the eggs, and mix until well blended. Pour half of the cheesecake batter over the crust. Sprinkle with cinnamon chips. Spoon the remaining batter over the cinnamon chips.

To create the cinnamon swirl: In a small bowl, stir together the butter, brown sugar, and cinnamon. Transfer the mixture to a squeeze bottle or a piping bag with a small tip cut off. Pipe the cinnamon mixture in a large swirl over the cheesecake.

To make the cheesecake: Place the springform pan on a baking sheet, and bake for 1 hour, or until the edges of the cheesecake are set and the center is still slightly jiggly. Turn off the oven and crack the oven door; let the cheesecake sit in the oven until the oven is cool. (This helps prevent cracks from forming in the cheesecake.)

Remove the cheesecake from the oven; let it cool to room temperature. Cover and chill in the refrigerator for 4–6 hours, or overnight.

mississippi mud cheesecake

Here we have all the flavors of Mississippi Mud Cake—chocolate, pecans, and marshmallows—but with all the luxuriousness of cheesecake plus the classic fudgy icing on top and a chocolate cookie crust on the bottom.

SERVES 10

For the crust:

24 Oreos cookies (do not discard cream filling)

¼ cup butter, melted

For the cheesecake filling:

3 (8-ounce) packages cream cheese, room temperature

1 (6-ounce) container plain Greek yogurt

¾ cup granulated sugar

½ cup light brown sugar, packed

⅓ cup Hershey's Special Dark Cocoa Powder

1 teaspoon vanilla extract

½ teaspoon salt

4 large eggs

¼ cup whole milk

4 ounces dark chocolate, melted

½ cup chopped pecans

For the topping:

½ cup butter

6 tablespoons whole milk

3 tablespoons Hershey's Special Dark Cocoa Powder

1 teaspoon vanilla extract

3 cups confectioners' sugar

Mini marshmallows

To make the crust: Preheat the oven to 325°F. Grease a 9-inch springform pan with cooking spray. Wrap foil around the bottom of the pan to prevent leaks.

Place the Oreos in a food processor, and process until finely ground. Combine the crumbs and melted butter in a small bowl; stir until the crumbs are evenly coated. Press the crust mixture into the bottom of the prepared springform pan.

To make the filling: In a large bowl, beat the cream cheese on medium speed with an electric mixer until smooth. Add the yogurt, both sugars, cocoa powder, vanilla, and salt; mix on low until just blended. With the mixer running, add the eggs one at a time, mixing well on low speed after each addition. Add the milk, and mix well. Fold in the melted chocolate and the pecans. Pour the batter over the crust.

To make the cheesecake: Place the springform pan on a baking sheet. Bake for 1 hour to 1 hour and 15 minutes, or until the center of the cheesecake barely jiggles. Turn the oven off, crack the oven door, and let the cheesecake cool in the oven.

Once the cheesecake is cool, remove the foil from the bottom. Run a knife around the inside of the springform pan to gently loosen the cheesecake from the sides of the pan. Cover with plastic wrap, and chill in the refrigerator for 4–6 hours, or overnight.

To make the topping: Melt butter in a medium saucepan over medium heat. Once melted, add the milk and cocoa, stirring continuously for 2–3 minutes. Remove from the heat, and whisk in the vanilla and confectioners' sugar. Arrange the mini marshmallows in an even layer over the cheesecake. Pour the icing over the marshmallows until completely coated. Let the icing set for a few minutes before serving.

Store loosely covered in the refrigerator.

NOTE: Many cheesecake recipes call for a water bath (placing the springform pan in a rectangular pan and filling it with enough water to reach about halfway up the sides of the springform pan) to help prevent cracks from forming in the top of the cheesecake. This recipe omits the water bath because the cheesecake will be covered with marshmallows and fudge frosting. If any cracks form while baking, they won't be visible once the cheesecake is finished. If you'd like to use a water bath, place the springform pan in a rectangular pan. Place in the oven, and then use a measuring cup to pour water into the rectangular pan. Bake as directed.

coconut–lemon meringue cheesecake

I tend to forget how much I love lemon desserts. Lemon brings vibrant, lively flavor to this lush cheesecake, especially with the lemon curd swirled right into the top. Finish it with toasty meringue for a luscious twist on everyone's favorite lemon pie.

SERVES 10

For the crust:

1¼ cups graham cracker crumbs

¼ cup shredded coconut

6 tablespoons butter, melted

For the filling:

3 (8-ounce) packages cream cheese, softened

1 (6-ounce) container coconut Greek yogurt

¾ cup granulated sugar

1 teaspoon coconut extract

1 cup lemon curd, divided

4 large eggs

⅓ cup shredded coconut

For the meringue:

3 large egg whites

½ teaspoon cream of tartar

3 tablespoons granulated sugar

½ teaspoon coconut extract

To make the crust: Preheat the oven to 350°F. Spray a 9-inch springform pan with cooking spray.

Combine the graham cracker crumbs and coconut in a food processor. Pulse until the coconut is finely ground. Transfer the mixture to a medium-size bowl, and stir in the melted butter. Press the crust into the bottom of the prepared pan. Set aside.

To make the filling: In a large bowl, beat the cream cheese and yogurt on medium-high speed with an electric mixer until smooth. Add the sugar, coconut extract, and ½ cup lemon curd; mix until well blended. Add the eggs and mix well. Fold in the shredded coconut.

To make the cheesecake: Pour the cheesecake filling over the crust. Drop small dollops of the remaining lemon curd over the filling. Use a toothpick to swirl the lemon curd into the cheesecake.

Place the springform pan on a baking sheet and bake for 1 hour. Turn the oven off, and let the cheesecake sit for 1 more hour. Remove from the oven and let cool completely. Cover and chill in the refrigerator for 4–6 hours, or overnight.

To make the meringue: Place the egg whites and cream of tartar in a medium-size bowl or the bowl of a stand mixer. Whip on high speed until frothy. With the mixer running, add the sugar 1 tablespoon at a time, and then add the coconut extract. Continue whipping until stiff peaks form. Spread the meringue over the chilled cheesecake.

You can toast the meringue with a kitchen torch, or use the broiler of your oven, Preheat the broiler, and place the cheesecake on a baking sheet. Broil until the top of the meringue is toasty.

Store loosely covered in the refrigerator until ready to serve.

elvis cheesecake

This has to be one of my top three favorite cheesecakes I've ever made. The creamy filling is a peanut butter lover's dream and is topped with sliced bananas coated in cinnamon and sugar, making it a cheesecake fit for the King!

SERVES 8–10

For the crust:

1½ cups cinnamon graham cracker crumbs

½ cup butter, melted

For the cheesecake:

3 (8-ounce) packages cream cheese

1 cup creamy peanut butter

¾ cup plus 3 tablespoons granulated sugar, divided

4 large eggs

1 teaspoon vanilla extract

⅓ cup whole milk

1 teaspoon ground cinnamon

3 large bananas, thinly sliced

To make the crust: Preheat the oven to 350°F. Lightly grease a 9-inch springform pan.

Stir together the crumbs and butter until evenly coated. Press into the bottom of the springform pan. Set aside.

To make the cheesecake: In a large bowl, beat the cream cheese on medium speed with an electric mixer until smooth. Add the peanut butter and ¾ cup sugar; mix well. With the mixer running, add the eggs one at a time, mixing well between each addition. Add the vanilla and milk; mix until incorporated. Pour the batter over the crust in the springform pan.

Stir together the 3 tablespoons sugar and the ground cinnamon. Sprinkle evenly over the sliced bananas, turn, and sprinkle the other sides. Carefully arrange the bananas over the cheesecake in the pan until the top is covered.

Place the springform pan on a baking sheet, and bake for 1 hour. Turn off the oven, crack the oven door, and let the cheesecake sit inside the oven for 1 more hour. Remove from the oven, and cool to room temperature. Cover and chill 4–6 hours, or overnight.

brownie-bottomed praline cheesecakes

These little cheesecakes are perfect for parties! They're less fussy and bake faster than a traditional cheesecake, and the praline sauce adds the perfect amount of crunch.

MAKES 24

For the praline sauce:

4 tablespoons butter

½ cup packed dark brown sugar

2 tablespoons heavy whipping cream (or whole milk)

½ teaspoon vanilla extract

Pinch of salt

½ cup chopped pecans

For the brownie:

½ cup butter, diced

½ cup milk chocolate chips

1 cup granulated sugar

¼ cup unsweetened cocoa powder

⅓ cup whole milk

2 large eggs

1 teaspoon vanilla extract

¾ cup all-purpose flour

For the cheesecake:

2 (8-ounce) packages cream cheese, softened

1 (6-ounce) container plain Greek yogurt

¾ cup granulated sugar

3 large eggs

1 teaspoon vanilla extract

To make the praline sauce: Melt the butter in a medium saucepan over medium heat. Add the dark brown sugar, and whisk continuously until it melts and the mixture begins to boil, about 5 minutes. Stir in the cream, vanilla, salt, and pecans. Let the sauce cool completely. (The sauce can be made a day in advance. Store in an airtight container at room temperature.)

Preheat the oven to 350°F. Line two 12-cup muffin pans with paper liners.

To make the brownie batter: Combine the butter and chocolate chips in a large microwave-safe bowl. Microwave in 30-second intervals, stirring after each, until melted and smooth. Whisk in the sugar, unsweetened cocoa powder, and milk. Add the eggs and vanilla, whisking to combine. Whisk in the flour.

To make the cheesecake filling: In a medium bowl, beat the cream cheese with an electric mixer on medium speed until smooth. Add the yogurt and sugar; mix well. Add the eggs and vanilla; mix until well blended.

To assemble the cheesecakes: Spoon the brownie batter into the bottom of each muffin cup, just until the bottoms are covered. Spoon the cheesecake over the brownie batter until the muffin cups are about half full. Drizzle with ½ to 1 tablespoon praline sauce, and lightly swirl with a toothpick. Spoon in the remaining cheesecake batter until the cups are about two-thirds full. Drizzle with more praline sauce, and swirl with a toothpick. Bake 30–35 minutes, or until the edges are set and the centers are just slightly jiggly. Let cool to room temperature. Cover and chill 4–6 hours in the refrigerator.

frozen peanut butter cheesecake

You can't go wrong with a cool and creamy peanut butter pie. This one has a little extra crunch in the crust from crispy rice cereal! It's perfect topped with a nice dose of whipped cream and silky peanut butter sauce.

SERVES 8

For the peanut butter sauce:

¼ cup creamy peanut butter

¼ cup heavy whipping cream

2 tablespoons honey

2 tablespoons light corn syrup

Pinch of salt

½ teaspoon vanilla extract

For the crust:

1 cup graham cracker crumbs

½ cup honey-roasted peanuts

1 cup crispy rice cereal

6 tablespoons butter, melted

For the peanut butter filling:

1 (8-ounce) package cream cheese, softened

1 (6-ounce) container plain Greek yogurt

1 cup creamy peanut butter

1 cup confectioners' sugar

1 teaspoon vanilla extract

1½ cups heavy whipping cream

For the garnish:

Peanut Butter Sauce

Honey-roasted peanuts, chopped

Whipped Cream

To make the peanut butter sauce: Combine the peanut butter, cream, honey, corn syrup, and salt in a small saucepan over medium heat. Cook, stirring slowly, until the mixture is smooth, about 5–8 minutes. Remove from the heat, stir in the vanilla, and cool completely. (Peanut butter sauce can be made a few days in advance. Store covered in the refrigerator, and allow it to come to room temperature before using.)

To make the crust: Preheat the oven to 350°F. Combine the graham cracker crumbs and peanuts in a food processor. Process until finely ground. Transfer the crumbs to a large bowl. Add the cereal and butter; stir well. Press the crust mixture into the bottom and up the sides of an 8-inch pie plate. Bake 12 minutes. Remove from the oven and cool completely. Pour 1 cup of the peanut butter sauce into the pie crust. Transfer to the refrigerator while preparing the filling.

To make the filling: In a large bowl, beat the cream cheese on medium speed with an electric mixer until smooth. Add the yogurt and peanut butter; mix until well blended. Add the confectioners' sugar and vanilla, and mix until combined. In the bowl of a stand mixer using the whisk attachment, whip the heavy cream on high speed until stiff peaks form. Fold the whipped cream into the peanut butter mixture.

To make the cheesecake: Remove the crust from the refrigerator, and spread the filling evenly over the peanut butter sauce. Drizzle the top of the cheesecake with the remaining peanut butter sauce. Chill 3–4 hours before serving. Garnish with additional whipped cream, if desired, and sprinkle with chopped peanuts. Store loosely covered in the refrigerator.

Pies & Tarts

peaches and cream tart

If you're looking for a dessert with an easy yet impressive presentation, you're sure to stun your guests with this Peaches and Cream Tart. Don't let the decoration intimidate you! If the peaches are difficult to fold in the center, microwave them in a bowl of water in 30-second intervals just until pliable.

SERVES 8

For the shortbread tart crust:

12 tablespoons butter, cold and diced

¾ cup confectioners' sugar

2 egg yolks

2 cups all-purpose flour

1 tablespoon vanilla extract

Pinch of salt

For the whipped honey-mascarpone filling:

1 (8-ounce) package mascarpone cheese

⅓ cup honey

1 tablespoon vanilla bean paste (or vanilla extract)

1 cup heavy whipping cream

3 large peaches, thinly sliced

To make the shortbread crust: Combine the butter, confectioners' sugar, and egg yolks in a food processor. Process until mostly smooth with little flecks of butter throughout. Add the flour, vanilla, and salt. Process until a dough forms; transfer to a sheet of plastic wrap. Shape the tart dough into a circle, and wrap with plastic wrap. Chill in the refrigerator for at least 1 hour.

Let the tart dough thaw for 5–10 minutes. Preheat the oven to 350°F. Lightly grease a 9-inch tart pan with nonstick spray. Sprinkle a clean work surface with flour. Roll the tart dough into a 12-inch circle. Gently fit the tart dough in the tart pan, and prick the bottom of the tart all over with a fork. Lay a piece of parchment over the tart crust, and fill it with pie weights (or dried beans). Bake for 15 minutes, then remove the pie weights and paper. Bake for an additional 10 minutes, or until the crust is golden brown. Remove from the oven, and let the crust cool completely.

To make the filling: In a medium bowl, beat the mascarpone cheese and honey with an electric mixer on medium speed until smooth. Add the vanilla bean paste, and mix well. Add the heavy cream, and whip on high speed until stiff peaks form.

To make the pie: Spread the filling into the cooled tart shell. Arrange the sliced peaches over the filling, starting at the outside edge and working inward. Store the tart loosely covered in the refrigerator. Best served the same day.

classic chocolate cream pie

As someone who is more of a chocolate dessert person than a fruit dessert person, this chocolate cream pie is one of my go-to recipes. The pudding calls for semisweet chocolate, but feel free to use your favorite! Milk or dark chocolate would be just as rich and wonderful.

SERVES 8

For the chocolate pudding:

3 large egg yolks, lightly beaten

¾ cup granulated sugar

4 tablespoons unsweetened cocoa powder

2 ounces chopped semi-sweet chocolate

2 tablespoons cornstarch

2 cups heavy whipping cream

1 teaspoon vanilla extract

For the chocolate cookie crust:

28 chocolate sandwich cookies

6 tablespoons butter, melted

For the whipped cream:

1½ cups heavy whipping cream

2 tablespoons confectioners' sugar

½ teaspoon vanilla extract

For the garnishes:

Chocolate curls

Chocolate shavings

To make the pudding: Place the egg yolks in a small bowl, and set aside. In a medium saucepan over medium heat, combine the sugar, cocoa powder, chocolate, cornstarch, cream, and vanilla. Cook, whisking slowly until the sugar and chocolate melt. The mixture should be thoroughly heated but not boiling. Add about 1/4 cup of the mixture to the egg yolks, and whisk quickly to temper the eggs. Immediately add the egg mixture back to the saucepan, and continue whisking quickly to prevent the eggs from scrambling. Whisk until the mixture thickens into the consistency of pudding and coats the back of a rubber spatula or wooden spoon, about 5–10 minutes.

Remove the saucepan from the heat, and immediately cover the top of the pudding with clear plastic wrap (directly on the surface of the pudding), poking a few holes in the wrap with a knife. Let the pudding cool at room temperature for about an hour. Then transfer to the refrigerator, and chill 2–3 hours, or overnight.

To make the crust: Preheat the oven to 350°F. Place the chocolate cookies in a food processor, and process them into fine crumbs. Stir in the butter until the crumbs are evenly coated. Press the crust mixture into the bottom and about 1 inch up the sides of a pie plate. Bake 12 minutes, then set aside to cool completely.

To make the whipped cream: Place the cream, confectioners' sugar, and vanilla in a large bowl or the bowl of a stand mixer. Whip on high speed until stiff peaks form.

To assemble the pie: Spoon the pudding into the cooled pie crust. Spread the pudding evenly with a spoon or rubber spatula. Spread the whipped cream over the pudding, and garnish with chocolate curls or shavings. Store loosely covered in the refrigerator until ready to serve.

peanut butter chess pie

It seems like almost everyone has a chess pie recipe passed down from their grandmother. It's such a Southern classic, and for a good reason! The filling is super creamy, easy to whip up, and even easier to devour.

SERVES 8

For the pie crust:

1½ cups all-purpose flour

2 tablespoons sugar

½ teaspoon salt

6 tablespoons cold butter

6 tablespoons cold water

1 large egg

1 tablespoon whole milk

For the pie filling:

2 cups granulated sugar

4 large eggs, slightly beaten

⅔ cup evaporated milk

⅔ cup peanut butter

1 teaspoon vanilla extract

Pinch of salt

¼ cup butter, melted

For the garnish:

Ice cream

Chocolate sauce

Chopped peanuts

To make the pie crust: Combine the flour, sugar, and salt in a food processor. Add the butter and pulse until crumbly. With the processor running, add the water 1 tablespoon at a time until the dough comes together and forms a ball. Turn out onto a sheet of plastic wrap, and shape into a ball. Chill for 30 minutes. On a lightly floured surface, turn out the dough, and roll it into a 12-inch circle. Lift the dough using a rolling pin (if the dough is hard to work with, return it to the refrigerator to help it firm up a bit), and lay it over a lightly greased 9-inch pie plate. Gently press the dough into the pie plate. Trim and flute the edges. Beat the egg and milk with a fork until pale and frothy. Lightly brush the egg wash over the edges of the pie crust.

To make the filling: Combine the sugar, eggs, evaporated milk, peanut butter, vanilla, and salt in a large bowl. Mix on medium-high speed with an electric mixer until well blended. Add the butter and mix well.

To assemble the pie: Pour the filling into the prepared pie crust. Bake 20 minutes, then tent a sheet of aluminum foil over the pie. Continue baking for another 25 minutes, or until the center is set and the top is slightly crackled. Remove from the oven; let cool. This pie is best served slightly warm. Top with ice cream, chocolate sauce, and peanuts if desired.

tropical key lime pie

Is there anything easier than a Key lime pie? This one has been dressed up with macadamia nuts and coconut in the crust with pineapple juice added to the zesty Key lime juice in the filling. Every bite is full of sweet summer flavor.

SERVES 8–10

For the crust:

¼ cups graham cracker crumbs

¾ cup toasted coconut

½ cup macadamia nuts

1 tablespoon packed light brown sugar

6 tablespoons butter, melted

For the filling:

4 large egg yolks

1½ cups sweetened condensed milk

½ cup bottled Key lime juice

½ cup pineapple juice

1 tablespoon lime zest

For the garnish:

Toasted coconut

Lime wedges

To make the crust: Preheat the oven to 350°F. Lightly grease a pie plate with cooking spray. Combine the graham cracker crumbs, toasted coconut, macadamia nuts, and brown sugar in a food processor. Process until finely ground. Stir together the crust mixture with the melted butter until the crumbs are evenly coated. Press into the bottom and up the sides of the pie plate. Bake 10 minutes; remove from oven.

To make the filling: In a large bowl, whip the egg yolks with an electric mixer until thickened and lighter in color. Add the sweetened condensed milk, and mix until well blended. Add the Key lime juice, pineapple juice, and lime zest; mix well.

To make the pie: Pour the filling into the pie crust, and bake 15 minutes. Remove the pie from the oven. Cool it at room temperature for 30 minutes, then transfer it to the refrigerator to cool completely. Garnish the pie with toasted coconut and lime wedges. Store covered in the refrigerator.

apple-pecan slab pie

Get the best of both pies! This pie filling is so easy and simple to make. Just toss some apples together with pecans, brown sugar, and spices, and then bake.

SERVES 12

For the crust:

3 cups all-purpose flour

3 tablespoons granulated sugar

½ teaspoon salt

½ cup cold butter, diced

¼ cup vegetable shortening

½ cup cold water

For the filling:

5 large Granny Smith apples, peeled and diced

½ cup granulated sugar

¼ cup packed light brown sugar

3 tablespoons all-purpose flour

1 teaspoon ground cinnamon

1 teaspoon cornstarch

¼ teaspoon ground nutmeg

¾ cup finely chopped pecans

Pinch of salt

For the top crust:

1 large egg, lightly beaten

1 tablespoon whole milk

1 tablespoon raw sugar

For the garnish:

Vanilla ice cream (optional)

To make the pie crust: Combine the flour, sugar, and salt in a food processor. Add the butter and shortening, and pulse until crumbly. With the processor running, add the water 1 tablespoon at a time until the dough comes together and forms a ball. Divide the dough into two balls, shape them into circles, and wrap them with plastic wrap. Chill in the refrigerator 30 minutes. On a lightly floured surface, roll one circle of dough into a 15-inch rectangle. Lift the dough using a rolling pin, and lay it on a 9 X 15-inch greased or non-stick baking sheet.

To make the filling: Stir together the filling ingredients until the apples and pecans are evenly coated.

To assemble the pie: Spoon the filling over the crust. Beat the egg and milk with a fork until pale and frothy. Brush the egg wash over the edges of the pie crust.

Remove the second dough from the refrigerator. On a well-floured surface, roll the dough into a 15-inch rectangle. Using a pizza cutter, cut the dough into uniform strips. Arrange the strips in a lattice pattern over the pie filling, pressing the edges of the dough together to seal. Brush the egg wash over the lattice crust. Sprinkle the crust with raw sugar, if desired.

Bake 40–45 minutes, or until the crust is golden brown and the filling is bubbly. Let cool slightly before slicing and serving. Serve with vanilla ice cream, if desired.

chocolate turtle pecan pie

Think about all the reasons why you love pecan pie, and then think about adding fudgy chocolate to the mix. This pie is best served warm with a scoop of ice cream.

SERVES 8–10

For the all-butter pie crust:

1½ cups all-purpose flour

2 tablespoons sugar

½ teaspoon salt

6 tablespoons cold butter

6 tablespoons cold water

1 large egg

1 tablespoon whole milk

For the pie filling:

1 cup light corn syrup

3 large eggs

1 cup granulated sugar

½ cup unsweetened cocoa powder

2 tablespoons butter, melted

1 teaspoon vanilla extract

1 cup chopped pecans

2 cups pecan halves

½ cup salted caramel sauce

To make the pie crust: Combine the flour, sugar, and salt in a food processor. Add the butter, and pulse until crumbly. With the processor running, add water 1 tablespoon at a time until the dough comes together and forms a ball. Turn out the dough onto a sheet of plastic wrap, and shape into a ball. Chill for 30 minutes.

On a lightly floured surface, turn out the dough, and roll into a 12-inch circle. Lift the dough using a rolling pin (if dough is hard to work with, return it to the refrigerator to help it firm up a bit), and lay it over a lightly greased 9-inch pie plate. Gently press the dough into the pie plate, and flute the edges. Beat the egg and milk with a fork until pale and frothy. Brush the egg wash over the edges of the pie crust.

To make the pie filling: Preheat the oven to 350°F. In a large bowl, combine the corn syrup, eggs, sugar, and cocoa powder. Stir until well blended. Add the melted butter, vanilla, and chopped pecans, and mix well.

To assemble the pie: Pour the pie filling into the pie crust. Arrange the pecan halves over the filling. Bake the pie for 1 hour. Remove from the oven and cool slightly. Drizzle with caramel sauce before serving.

birthday buttermilk pie

As the person known for making birthday cakes, I had to give this simple buttermilk pie a colorful birthday twist. There are sprinkles in the filling and baked right into the pie crust!

SERVES 8

For the confetti crust:

1½ cups all-purpose flour

2 tablespoons sugar

½ teaspoon salt

6 tablespoons cold butter

6 tablespoons cold water

⅓ cup rainbow jimmies

1 large egg

1 tablespoon whole milk

For the pie filling:

3 large eggs

½ cup butter, very soft

1½ cups granulated sugar

3 tablespoons flour

1 cup buttermilk

½ cup sour cream

1 tablespoon vanilla extract

½ cup rainbow jimmies, divided

For the garnishes (optional):

Confectioners' sugar

Whipped cream or ice cream

To make the pie crust: Combine the flour, sugar, and salt in a food processor. Add the butter, and pulse until crumbly. With the processor running, add the water 1 tablespoon at a time until the dough comes together and forms a ball. Remove the blade from the food processor bowl, and fold in the sprinkles with a rubber spatula. Turn out the dough onto a sheet of plastic wrap, and shape it into a circle. Chill for 30 minutes.

Preheat the oven to 350°F. On a lightly floured surface, turn out the dough, and roll into a 12-inch circle. Lift the dough using a rolling pin (if dough is hard to work with, return to the refrigerator to help it firm up a bit), and lay it over a lightly greased 9-inch pie plate. Gently press the dough into the pie plate and flute the edges. Beat the egg and milk with a fork until pale and frothy. Brush the egg wash over the edges of the pie crust.

To make the pie filling: In a medium bowl, beat the eggs on medium-speed with an electric mixer until foamy. Add the butter, sugar, and flour, and mix until well blended. Add the buttermilk, sour cream, and vanilla; mix well. Stir in half of the sprinkles.

To assemble the pie: Pour the filling into the prepared pie crust. Sprinkle with the remaining sprinkles.

Bake 45 minutes, tenting with foil about halfway through to prevent burning the crust. Bake until the edges of the pie are set and the center jiggles only slightly. Remove from the oven, and cool completely before serving. Top with confectioners sugar, whipped cream, or ice cream if desired.

salted honey pecan pie
with Browned Butter Crust

This pie is a combination of a custard-like salted honey pie and, of course, a pecan pie. It's sweet with a slight caramel flavor while still maintaining that classic pecan pie feeling.

SERVES 8–10

For the browned butter crust:

6 tablespoons butter

1½ cups all-purpose flour

2 tablespoons granulated sugar

½ teaspoon salt

2 tablespoons vegetable shortening

6 tablespoons cold water

1 large egg

1 tablespoon whole milk

For the pie filling:

¼ cup butter

¾ cup granulated sugar

¾ cup honey

½ teaspoon salt

3 tablespoons cornmeal

1 teaspoon white vinegar

3 large eggs

½ cup heavy whipping cream

1 teaspoon vanilla bean paste

1½ cups chopped pecans

½ tablespoon flaky sea salt

To make the browned butter: Melt the butter in a small saucepan over medium heat. Bring to a simmer; let the butter cook, swirling the saucepan occasionally, until the milk solids have browned, about 8–10 minutes. Remove from the heat, and let the butter cool completely. Pour browned butter into a small bowl, making sure to scrape all the browned bits, and chill in the freezer until solid. Cut into small cubes.

To make the pie crust: Combine the flour, sugar, and salt in a food processor. Add the browned butter and vegetable shortening; pulse until crumbly. With the processor running, add water 1 tablespoon at a time until the dough comes together and forms a ball. Turn out the dough onto a sheet of plastic wrap, and shape into a ball. Chill for 30 minutes. On a lightly floured surface, turn out the dough, and roll it into a 12-inch circle. Lift the dough using a rolling pin (if dough is hard to work with, return it to the refrigerator to help it firm up a bit), and lay it over a lightly greased 9-inch pie plate. Gently press the dough into the pie plate, and flute the edges. Beat the egg and milk with a fork until pale and frothy. Brush the egg wash over the edges of the pie crust.

To make the pie filling: Preheat the oven to 375°F. Brown the butter again using the same method as for the crust. Instead of chilling the butter, this time just let it cool to almost room temperature but still melted. Whisk together the melted browned butter, sugar, honey, salt, cornmeal, and vinegar. Add the eggs one at a time, whisking well after each addition. Whisk in the cream and vanilla. Fold in the pecans.

To assemble the pie: Pour the filling into the prepared pie crust. Place the pie in the oven, and bake 45–50 minutes, or until the crust is golden brown and the filling is only slightly jiggly in the center. (Tent the pie with foil if the crust begins to brown too much.) Remove the pie from the oven and cool. Sprinkle with flaky sea salt.

muscadine hull pie

If you really want to make something Southern, muscadines are about as Southern as you can get. This pie came about as a way to use the hulls, while the pulp and juices are typically used in things like jam and wine. This recipe cooks the hulls with the pulp, which results in a sweet and tart filling that is similar to sour cherries.

SERVES 8

For the filling:

4 cups fresh muscadines

2 tablespoons lemon juice

1 cup granulated sugar

¼ cup packed light brown sugar

1 tablespoon cornstarch

Pinch of salt

1 teaspoon vanilla extract

For the double pie crust:

2 cups all-purpose flour

2 tablespoons granulated sugar

½ teaspoon salt

1 cup cold butter, diced

½ cup cold water

1 large egg

1 tablespoon whole milk

For garnish:

Ice cream (optional)

To make the pie filling: Cut the muscadines in half, press the pulp from the hulls, and remove the seeds. Combine the hulls, pulp, and lemon juice in a large saucepan over medium-high heat. Bring the mixture to a boil, then reduce to a simmer. Add both sugars, cornstarch, salt, and vanilla. Cook for 35–40 minutes, or until the hulls are tender.

To make the pie crust: While the filling is cooking, make the pie crust. Combine the flour, sugar, and salt in a food processor. Add the butter, and pulse until crumbly. With the processor running, add the water 1 tablespoon at a time until the dough comes together and forms a ball. Divide the dough in half, and wrap each with plastic wrap. Chill for 30 minutes.

To assemble the pie: When ready to bake the pie, preheat the oven to 350°F. Turn out one ball of dough on a well-floured surface, and roll into a 12-inch circle. Lift the dough using a rolling pin, and lay it over a lightly greased 9-inch pie plate. Gently press the dough into the pie plate, and flute the edges. Beat the egg and milk with a fork until pale and frothy. Brush the egg wash over the edges of the pie crust. Pour the muscadine pie filling into the crust. Roll out the remaining dough into a 10-inch circle on a well-floured surface, and cut into even strips with a pizza cutter. Arrange the strips into a lattice crust over the filling, and trim as necessary.

Place the pie plate on a baking sheet, and bake 40–45 minutes. (Tent the pie with a piece of aluminum foil if the crust begins to brown too quickly.) Remove the pie from the oven, and let it cool. Serve warm with ice cream, if desired.

fried berry hand pies

These pies are best eaten warm with a generous dusting of confectioners' sugar. Feel free to bake them on a sheet pan if you'd rather not fry them. There's nothing better than your very own warm little pie on a crisp autumn day.

MAKES 10–12

For the buttermilk crust:

1½ cups all-purpose flour

2 tablespoons granulated sugar

½ teaspoon salt

4 tablespoons butter, cold and diced

2 tablespoons vegetable shortening

4–6 tablespoons buttermilk

For the berry filling:

1 cup diced strawberries

1 cup raspberries

1 cup blueberries

1 teaspoon almond extract

⅓ cup granulated sugar

¼ cup all-purpose flour

½ teaspoon ground cinnamon

2–3 tablespoons water

Vegetable oil, for frying

Confectioners' sugar, for garnish

To make the pie crust: To make the pie crust, combine the flour, sugar, and salt in a food processor. Add the butter and shortening; pulse until crumbly. With the processor running, add the buttermilk 1 tablespoon at a time until the dough comes together and forms a ball. Turn out the dough onto a sheet of plastic wrap, and shape into a ball. Chill for 30 minutes.

To make the pie filling: Stir together the berries, almond extract, sugar, flour, and cinnamon.

To assemble the pies: On a lightly floured surface, turn out the dough, and roll it out until it is about ¼-inch thick. Using a 5- to 6-inch round cookie cutter, cut circles out of the pie dough. Place a heaping tablespoon of pie filling in the center of each circle. Lightly brush water around the edges, fold the dough over to create a half circle, and crimp the edges together with a fork. Gather the dough scraps, and reroll the pie dough, repeating this process until all the dough has been used. (If the dough becomes too soft to work with, return it to the refrigerator for 10 minutes to firm up.)

When ready to fry, heat 2 inches of oil in a large, heavy-bottomed pot until a candy thermometer reaches 350°F. Fry three or four pies at a time for 3–4 minutes per side, or until golden brown. Remove with a slotted spoon, and transfer to a wire rack. Dust with confectioners' sugar.

If you prefer to bake these pies, preheat the oven to 350°F. Place pies on a parchment paper-lined baking sheet and bake 18–20 minutes, or until crust is golden brown.

blueberry-lemon tart

Adding a beautiful drizzle of blueberry sauce to a creamy, dreamy lemon tart makes for one fancy upgrade! You can even substitute your favorite berries for the blueberries.

SERVES 8

For the blueberry sauce:

1 cup blueberries

¼ cup granulated sugar

½ cup water

For the crust:

1½ cups graham cracker crumbs

½ cup butter, melted

For the lemon filling:

4 large egg yolks

1½ cups sweetened condensed milk

½ cup lemon juice

1 tablespoon lemon zest

For the garnishes:

Toasted coconut

Lime wedges

To make the blueberry sauce: Place the blueberries in a small blender or food processor. Blend until smooth. Combine the blueberry puree, sugar, and water in a medium saucepan over medium heat. Bring to a low boil, and stir slowly until the sugar dissolves. Reduce to a simmer and cook, stirring occasionally, until the mixture thickens to a syrup-like consistency, about 10–15 minutes. Remove from the heat, and set aside to cool completely. (The blueberry sauce can be made in advance and kept in the refrigerator in a sealed container for 1–2 days.)

To make the crust: Preheat the oven to 350°F. Stir together the graham cracker crumbs and butter in a small bowl. Press into a lightly greased 9-inch tart pan. Bake 10 minutes. Remove from the oven.

To make the filling: In a medium bowl, whip the egg yolks with an electric mixer until thickened and lighter in color. Add the sweetened condensed milk, and mix until well blended. Add the lemon juice and lemon zest; mix well.

To assemble the tart: Pour the filling into baked pie crust. Pipe or drizzle the blueberry sauce in horizontal lines over the filling. Use a toothpick to swirl the sauce into the filling, moving in straight lines perpendicular to the blueberry sauce.

Return to the oven, and bake 15 minutes. Cool the tart at room temperature for 30 minutes, then transfer it to the refrigerator to cool completely. Garnish with toasted coconut and lime wedges. Store covered in the refrigerator.

kentucky derby pie

Derby Pie is essentially pecan pie with the addition of chocolate and bourbon. Here I've also added a touch of maple syrup and topped it with bourbon whipped cream for a little extra of that boozy flavor.

SERVES 8

For the crust:

1½ cups all-purpose flour

2 tablespoons sugar

½ teaspoon salt

6 tablespoons cold butter

6 tablespoons cold water

1 large egg

1 tablespoon whole milk

For the pie filling:

½ cup butter, softened

1 cup granulated sugar

¼ cup pure maple syrup

2 large eggs

1 teaspoon vanilla extract

2 tablespoons bourbon

½ cup all-purpose flour

½ teaspoon salt

1 cup semisweet chocolate chips

1 cup chopped pecans

2 cups pecan halves

For the bourbon-maple whipped cream:

1 cup heavy whipping cream

1 tablespoon bourbon

2 tablespoons pure maple syrup

To make the pie crust: Combine the flour, sugar, and salt in a food processor. Add the butter, and pulse until crumbly. With the processor running, add the water 1 tablespoon at a time until the dough comes together and forms a ball. Turn out the dough onto a sheet of plastic wrap, and shape it into a disc. Chill for 30 minutes. On a lightly floured surface, turn out the dough, and roll it into a 12-inch circle. Lift the dough using a rolling pin (if the dough is hard to work with, return it to the refrigerator to help it firm up a bit), and lay it over a lightly greased 9-inch pie plate. Gently press the dough into the pie plate, and flute the edges. Beat the egg and milk with a fork until pale and frothy. Brush the egg wash over the edges of the pie crust.

To make the pie filling: Preheat the oven to 350°F. In a large bowl, beat the butter and sugar on medium-high speed with an electric mixer until fluffy. Add the maple syrup, eggs, vanilla, and bourbon. Mix well. Add the flour and salt; mix until well blended. Fold in the chocolate chips and chopped pecans.

To assemble the pie: Pour the pie filling into the prepared crust, and arrange the pecan halves over the top. Bake 45–50 minutes (tent with foil if the crust begins to brown too quickly), or until the pie is set around the edges and slightly jiggly in the center. Let the pie cool 1–2 hours before serving.

To make the whipped cream: In the bowl of a stand mixer using the whisk attachment, combine all the ingredients and mix on high speed until stiff peaks form. Serve with pie.

strawberry margarita tart

Yes, this tart has tequila in it. Like a great margarita, the filling is prepared with fresh strawberries and lime juice, and the saltiness comes from the pretzel crust.

SERVES 8

For the crust:

1 cup graham cracker crumbs

1 cup finely ground pretzel crumbs

2 tablespoons granulated sugar

6 tablespoons butter, melted

For the strawberry margarita filling:

3 cups sliced strawberries

¼ cup fresh lime juice

¼ cup tequila

1 cup granulated sugar

2 teaspoons cornstarch

2 tablespoons water

1 tablespoon lime zest

1½ cups heavy whipping cream

Sliced strawberries (about 2 cups)

For garnishes:

Whipped cream

Lime zest

To make the crust: Preheat the oven to 350°F. In a medium bowl, stir together all of the crust ingredients until evenly coated with melted butter. Press into a 9-inch tart pan. Bake 12 minutes; remove from the oven, and cool completely.

To make the filling: Add the strawberries to a blender, and blend until smooth. Combine the pureed strawberries, lime juice, tequila, and sugar in a medium saucepan over medium heat. Bring to a simmer, and reduce the heat to medium-low. Cook, stirring occasionally, until the sugar dissolves, about 5 minutes. Stir together the cornstarch and water; add to the saucepan. Continue cooking, stirring slowly, until the mixture thickens and resembles the consistency of jam. Remove from the heat; stir in the lime zest. Cool completely. (Place the mixture in the refrigerator to speed up cooling. The mixture will thicken as it cools.)

In the bowl of a stand mixer using the whisk attachment, whip the heavy cream on high speed until stiff peaks form. Fold the whipped cream into the strawberry mixture until well blended.

To assemble the tart: Spread the filling into the prepared crust. Arrange sliced strawberries over the tart. Top with additional whipped cream and sprinkle with lime zest. Loosely cover, and chill 2–3 hours in the refrigerator.

bourbon sweet potato pie
with Brown Sugar Streusel

Sweet potato pie is already a Thanksgiving favorite, but it's even better with a nice splash of bourbon and plenty of crumbly streusel! It'll be the hit of your holiday dessert table.

SERVES 8–10

For the crust:

1½ cups all-purpose flour

2 tablespoons packed light brown sugar

½ teaspoon salt

½ teaspoon cinnamon

6 tablespoons cold butter, cubed

6 tablespoons cold water

1 large egg

1 tablespoon whole milk

For the brown sugar streusel:

⅓ cup packed light brown sugar

1 cup all-purpose flour

½ teaspoon cinnamon

¼ teaspoon salt

½ cup finely chopped pecans

½ cup cold butter, cubed

To make the pie crust: Combine the flour, sugar, salt, and cinnamon in a food processor. Add the butter, and pulse until crumbly. With the processor running, add the water 1 tablespoon at a time until the dough comes together and forms a ball. Turn out the dough onto a sheet of plastic wrap, and shape into a disc. Chill for 30 minutes. On a lightly floured surface, turn out the dough, and roll into a 12-inch circle. Lift the dough using a rolling pin, and lay it over a lightly greased 9-inch pie plate. Gently press the dough into the pie plate, and flute the edges. Place the pie plate in the refrigerator while preparing the filling and crumble. Lightly whisk the egg and milk in a small bowl until combined. Reserve the egg wash until just before baking the pie.

To make the streusel: Combine all of the ingredients in a medium bowl. Use a pastry cutter or two knives to cut the butter into the dry ingredients until the mixture is crumbly. Set aside.

To make the pie filling: Preheat the oven to 350°F. Combine the mashed sweet potato, brown sugar, and corn syrup in a large bowl. Mix on medium speed with an electric mixer until blended. Add the bourbon, cinnamon, nutmeg, ginger, salt, and vanilla; mix well. Add the eggs and cream; mix until well blended.

To finish the pie: Lightly brush the egg wash over the edges of the pie crust. Pour the sweet potato filling into the crust. Top with an even layer of streusel. Place the pie plate on a baking sheet, and bake 20–25 minutes, or until the crust and streusel are golden brown. Tent the pie with a piece of aluminum foil, and bake 20–25 minutes longer, or until the edges are set and the center of the pie jiggles just slightly. Let the pie cool completely before serving.

For the pie filling:

3 cups cooked (and cooled), mashed sweet potato

¾ cup packed light brown sugar

¼ cup light corn syrup

¼ cup bourbon

1 teaspoon cinnamon

½ teaspoon nutmeg

¼ teaspoon ginger

¼ teaspoon salt

1 teaspoon vanilla extract

2 large eggs

¾ cup heavy whipping cream

mini chocolate chip pecan pies

These mini pies are the perfect single serving and are great for get-togethers and holiday parties. The extra-nutty flavor comes from toasty browned butter in the pie filling.

MAKES 12

For the crust:

1 double pie crust recipe
   (see page 171)

For the filling:

3 large eggs, lightly beaten

1 cup light corn syrup

½ cup granulated sugar

¼ cup packed light brown
   sugar

1 teaspoon vanilla extract

¼ teaspoon salt

¼ cup butter, browned and
   cooled but still melted

1½ cups chopped pecans

1 cup mini chocolate chips

1 cup pecan halves

To prepare the pies: Preheat the oven to 350°F. Lightly spray a 12-cup muffin pan with cooking spray. Roll out the pie crust on a well-floured surface. Using a 4-inch or 5-inch round cookie cutter, cut circles out of the dough, and press them into the prepared muffin pan. Transfer the pan to the refrigerator while preparing the filling.

To make the filling: Combine the eggs and corn syrup in a large bowl. Mix on medium speed with an electric mixer until just blended. Add both sugars, vanilla, and salt; mix until combined. Add the butter, and mix until smooth. Stir in the chopped pecans and chocolate chips.

To finish: Remove the pan from the refrigerator. Scoop the filling into each pie crust, filling each about three-quarters full. Arrange the pecan halves on top of each mini pie. Bake 35 minutes, or until the crust is golden brown and the filling is set. Remove from the oven and cool.

caramel apple rose tarts

Not only do these apple rose tarts have a beautiful presentation, they're also very easy to make and require minimal ingredients. The hardest part is waiting for them to bake before eating! If you don't have a mandoline, you can use a sharp knife.

MAKES 12

4 sweet apples, such as Honey Crisp

2 tablespoons lemon juice

2 packages puff pastry (4 sheets), thawed

¾ cup apple jam

1–2 tablespoons cinnamon

½–1 cup salted caramel sauce (homemade or store bought)

For garnish:
Confectioners' sugar

Preheat the oven to 350°F. Lightly grease a 12-cup muffin pan with cooking spray.

Cut the apples in half, and scoop out the seeds. Cut in half again, and thinly slice with a mandolin. Add the apple slices to a medium microwave-safe bowl, and fill with enough water to just cover the apples. Add the lemon juice, and microwave for 3 minutes. (This makes the apples more pliable and easier to roll up.) Drain and pat the apples dry.

On a lightly floured surface, unroll the puff pastry, working one sheet at a time, and roll with a rolling pin until flat and smooth. Cut into 2-inch strips (discarding the edges of the pastry if uneven), creating 12 strips total. Spread a very thin layer of apple jam on each strip of pastry, and sprinkle with cinnamon. Working one strip at a time, lay the apple slices along one edge, leaving the upper half of the apples exposed. Fold the bottom half of the pastry up and over the bottom half of the apples. Starting at one end, roll up the pastry, and place in the muffin pan. Repeat with the remaining strips.

Bake the tarts 35–40 minutes, or until the pastry is golden brown and the apples are beginning to brown along the edges. Remove from oven, and cool completely. Drizzle the tarts with caramel sauce, and dust with confectioners' sugar before serving.

coconut-pecan cream pie

The idea for this pie came to me via my grandmother, who makes wonderful coconut pies, and a family favorite: "mystery pecan pie." My version has a thin pecan pie layer on the bottom and a homemade coconut custard on top, plus a final layer of coconut whipped cream.

SERVES 8–10

For the crust:

1 recipe all-butter pie crust
(see page 170)

For the pecan pie layer:

⅓ cup light corn syrup

1 large egg

¼ cup granulated sugar

2 tablespoons packed light
brown sugar

1 teaspoon vanilla extract

1 cup chopped pecans

For the coconut custard:

3 large egg yolks, lightly
beaten

½ cup granulated sugar

2 tablespoons cornstarch

2 cups heavy cream

1 teaspoon coconut extract

1½ cups shredded coconut

For the coconut whipped
cream:

1½ cups heavy whipping
cream

3 tablespoons confectioners'
sugar

2 teaspoons coconut extract

For the garnishes:

Shredded coconut

Chopped pecans

Preheat the oven to 350°F. On a lightly floured surface, turn out the dough, and roll it into a 12-inch circle. Lift the dough using a rolling pin and lay it over a lightly greased 9-inch pie plate. Gently press the dough into the pie plate, and flute the edges.

To make the pecan pie layer: In a medium bowl, stir together all the ingredients. Pour into the prepared pie crust. Bake for 15 minutes. Remove from the oven and let cool completely.

To make the coconut custard: Place the egg yolks in a small bowl. Combine the sugar, cornstarch, and cream in a medium saucepan over medium heat. Stir constantly until the sugar has dissolved. Pour about ¼ cup of the mixture into the bowl with the egg yolks; whisk quickly to temper the yolks. Then pour the yolk mixture back into the saucepan, whisking to combine. Continue stirring for 5–10 minutes, or until the mixture becomes pudding-like in consistency and is thick enough to coat the back of a spoon. Remove from the heat, stir in coconut extract and shredded coconut, and immediately press a sheet of plastic wrap right onto the surface of the pudding. Poke a few holes through the plastic wrap, and let the custard cool 1–2 hours. Transfer to the refrigerator for another 1–2 hours. Once cool, spread the custard filling over the pecan pie layer.

To make the whipped cream: In the bowl of a stand mixer using the whisk attachment, combine the cream, confectioners' sugar, and extract. Whip on high speed until stiff peaks form. Spread over the pie, and sprinkle with coconut and pecans. Store the pie loosely covered in the refrigerator.

black and blueberry galette

Juicy summer berries make the perfect galettes! The pecan–whole wheat crust adds a touch of nutty flavor and Southern charm.

SERVES 8

For the pecan–whole wheat crust:

¾ cup chopped pecans

1½ cups whole wheat flour

3 tablespoons granulated sugar

½ teaspoon salt

½ cup cold butter, cubed

6 tablespoons cold water

For the filling:

1½ cups fresh blueberries

1½ cups fresh blackberries

¼ cup granulated sugar

1 tablespoon cornstarch

Juice and zest of 1 lemon

Pinch of ground cinnamon

Pinch of ground nutmeg

For the galette:

1 large egg

1 tablespoon water

2 tablespoons raw sugar

For the garnish:

Mint leaves

Ice cream

To make the crust: Place the pecans in a food processor. Pulse until finely ground. Add the flour, sugar, and salt. Pulse a couple times to blend. Add the butter, and process until the mixture is crumbly. With the food processor running, drizzle in the water until the dough comes together. Turn out the dough onto a sheet of plastic wrap, and shape the dough into a disc. Refrigerate 30 minutes.

To make the filling: In a large bowl, stir together the blueberries, blackberries, sugar, cornstarch, lemon juice, lemon zest, cinnamon, and nutmeg.

To assemble the galette: Preheat the oven to 350°F. Line a baking sheet with parchment paper. Turn out the dough onto a well-floured surface. Roll it into a 12-inch circle, and transfer it to the baking sheet. Spoon the filling into the center, and leave a 2-inch border around the edges. Fold the edges of crust over the filling, overlapping as necessary. Lightly beat the egg and water together, and brush it over the edges of the crust. Sprinkle with raw sugar.

Bake 30–35 minutes, or until the crust is golden brown. Remove from the oven, and let cool slightly. Garnish with mint leaves. Cut into wedges, and serve with ice cream, if desired.

Note: If using frozen berries, let the berries thaw, and then gently pat them dry with paper towels.

NO-BAKE GOODIES

watermelon-honeysuckle pops

These pops are flavored with some of my favorite local honeysuckle vodka and sweetened with a touch of honey as well. They're perfect and refreshing on those sweltering southern summer days.

MAKES 10

½ pound watermelon, cubed

¼ cup honey (not raw)

¼ cup honeysuckle vodka

¼ cup fresh lime juice

Place the watermelon in a blender, and blend until smooth. Combine 4 cups of the puree in a pitcher with the honey, honeysuckle vodka, and lime juice. Stir well. Pour into a 10-count ice pop mold, or use paper cups, and freeze for 30 minutes to 1 hour. Insert ice pop sticks, and freeze 4–6 additional hours, or until firm. To loosen the pops from the mold, dip it in warm water for 20–30 seconds.

peanut butter balls

Another one of my favorite recipes from my grandmother—classic peanut butter balls, which we always had around the holidays. No twists or spins for this recipe, just a classic.

MAKES 18–20

1½ cups creamy peanut butter

½ cup graham cracker crumbs

½ cup butter, cubed

1 teaspoon vanilla extract

¼ teaspoon salt

3 cups confectioners' sugar

2 (12-ounce) packages semisweet chocolate chips

¼ cup coconut oil

⅓ cup chopped peanuts (optional)

Combine the peanut butter, graham cracker crumbs, butter, vanilla, and salt in a large bowl. Mix with an electric mixer until smooth. Add the confectioners' sugar gradually until completely incorporated. Transfer the dough to the refrigerator, and chill for 30 minutes to 1 hour, or until the dough is firm enough to roll into balls.

Once the dough is firm, roll into 1-inch balls, and place on a sheet of parchment or waxed paper. Return the balls to the refrigerator until firm. Melt the chocolate and coconut oil in a microwave-safe dish in 30-second intervals, stirring between each, until smooth. Use a fork to drop the peanut butter balls one at a time into the chocolate. Gently stir until coated, lift with a fork, and let the excess chocolate drip back into the dish. Return the balls to the parchment paper. Sprinkle with chopped peanuts if desired. Repeat with the remaining peanut butter balls. (If the chocolate becomes too thick to dip, return the dish to the microwave for 10 seconds, and stir.) Transfer the peanut butter balls to the refrigerator until the chocolate is set. Store covered in the refrigerator.

bourbon balls

These sweet truffles are filled with chopped pecans, a little bit of spice, and a little bit of bourbon. Serve them during the holidays or package them for gifts!

MAKES 18–20

½ cup butter, softened

2 cups confectioners' sugar

¼ cup bourbon

2 tablespoons pure maple syrup

1 teaspoon vanilla extract

2 tablespoons unsweetened cocoa powder

Pinch of ground cinnamon

½ teaspoon salt

1 cup finely chopped pecans

1 (12-ounce) package semi-sweet chocolate chips

Pecan halves, toasted, for garnish

Flaky sea salt, for garnish

Chopped pecans, for garnish

In a large bowl, cream the butter on medium-high speed with an electric mixer. Add the confectioners' sugar, and mix until well blended. Add the bourbon, maple syrup, vanilla, cocoa powder, cinnamon, and salt. Mix well. Fold in the chopped pecans. Cover and chill in the refrigerator for 1 hour.

Once the mixture is firm, line a baking sheet with parchment or waxed paper. Roll the mixture into 1-inch balls, and place on the parchment. Return to the refrigerator until firm.

Microwave the chocolate chips in a microwave-safe dish in 30-second intervals, stirring well between each. Dip the bourbon balls in chocolate one at a time, letting the excess chocolate drip back into the bowl. Return the balls to the baking sheet. Immediately top each ball with 1 pecan half and a light sprinkle of sea salt and chopped pecans. Chill in the refrigerator until the chocolate is set. Store covered in the refrigerator.

strawberry delight pops

Strawberry Delight is one of those recipes that's delicious no matter what kind of berry or fruit you decide to use, and that is also true for these pops. Layer up the creamy filling, berry sauce, and crunchy granola for a cool treat.

MAKES 10

For the strawberry sauce:

2 cups chopped strawberries

¼ cup granulated sugar

½ cup plus 1 tablespoon water, divided

1 tablespoon cornstarch

For the filling:

1 (8-ounce) package cream cheese, room temperature

1 cup confectioners' sugar

⅓ cup strawberry sauce

1 cup heavy whipping cream

1½ cups granola (your favorite)

To make the sauce: Place the strawberries in a blender, and blend until pureed. Transfer to a medium saucepan over medium heat. Add the sugar and ½ cup water. Cook, stirring occasionally, until the mixture begins to simmer. In a separate bowl, stir together the cornstarch and 1 tablespoon water. Add to the saucepan. Stir until the mixture is thickened and syrupy. Remove from the heat; let the strawberry sauce cool completely.

To make the filling: In a medium bowl, beat the cream cheese on medium speed with an electric mixer until smooth. Add the confectioners' sugar, strawberry sauce, and whipping cream. Mix until well blended.

To make the pops: In an ice pop mold, or using paper cups, layer the granola, a drizzle of sauce, and some strawberry filling, repeating as necessary, until the molds are full. Freeze for about 30 minutes, then insert ice pop sticks. Freeze 3–4 hours, or until the pops are firm. Dip the mold in warm water for 20–30 seconds to loosen the pops.

no-churn blueberry crumble ice cream

I'm a pretty huge fan of no-churn ice creams because they're easy, take minimal effort, and don't require an ice cream maker. This ice cream swirls together a vanilla ice cream base, homemade blueberry sauce, and crumble topping.

SERVES 6–8

For the blueberry jelly:

2 cups fresh blueberries

¼ cup granulated sugar

1 tablespoon cornstarch

1 tablespoon water

1 teaspoon vanilla extract

For the crumble:

⅓ cup all-purpose flour

¼ cup old-fashioned oats

2 tablespoons granulated sugar

2 tablespoons packed light brown sugar

¼ teaspoon ground cinnamon

3 tablespoons butter

For the ice cream base:

1 (14-ounce) can sweetened condensed milk

4 ounces cream cheese, very soft

2 cups heavy whipping cream

To make the blueberry jelly: Add the blueberries to a blender, and blend until pureed. Transfer to a medium saucepan over medium heat; add sugar. Bring the mixture to a low boil, stirring slowly. Reduce the heat to a simmer. Stir together the cornstarch and water in a small bowl. Add to the blueberry mixture. Stir until the mixture begins to thicken. Let it cook for 8–10 minutes, stirring occasionally, until the mixture begins to resemble the consistency of jelly. Remove from heat; stir in the vanilla. Let the blueberry jelly cool completely before using. (Jelly can be made a day or two in advance and stored in an airtight container in the refrigerator until ready to use.)

To make the crumble: Preheat the oven to 350°F. Whisk together the flour, oats, sugars, and cinnamon. Cut in the butter with a pastry cutter or two knives until the mixture is crumbly. Spread in a 9-inch square baking dish, and bake 10–15 minutes, or until golden brown. Let cool completely.

To make the ice cream base: In a large bowl, mix together the sweetened condensed milk and cream cheese with an electric mixer until smooth. In the bowl of a stand mixer using the whisk attachment, whip the heavy cream on high speed until stiff peaks form. Fold the whipped cream into the cream cheese mixture.

To prepare the ice cream: Spoon half of the ice cream base into an 8-inch cake pan or 9 x 5-inch loaf pan. Dollop the ice cream with the desired amount of blueberry jelly, and swirl it into the ice cream with a knife or toothpick. Sprinkle with half of the crumbs. Repeat the layers one more time. Freeze 4–6 hours, or overnight.

no-churn watergate salad ice cream

Inspired by the classic Watergate fruit salad, this ice cream is a fun way to enjoy the sweet pistachio-flavored dish.

SERVES 8–10

For the ice cream base:

- 1 (14-ounce) can sweetened condensed milk
- 1 (4.5-ounce) package instant pistachio pudding mix
- 1 (8-ounce) can crushed pineapple in juice, drained and juice reserved
- ⅓ cup finely chopped pecans
- ¾ cup mini marshmallows
- 2 cups heavy whipping cream

For the garnishes:

Whipped cream

Chopped pecans

Maraschino cherries

In a large bowl, whisk together the sweetened condensed milk, pudding mix, and reserved pineapple juice. Stir in ⅓ cup crushed pineapple, the pecans, and marshmallows.

In the bowl of a stand mixer using the whisk attachment, whip the cream on medium-high speed until stiff peaks form. Fold the whipped cream into the ice cream base. Spoon the ice cream into a 9 × 5-inch loaf pan, and freeze 4–6 hours, or overnight. Garnish with whipped cream, pecans, and cherries.

easy peach cobbler ice cream

Similar to the blueberry crumble version, this ice cream is layered with homemade cobbler topping and chopped fresh peaches. Switch up the summer fruits and enjoy all season long.

SERVES 6–8

For the cobbler:

¼ cup butter, softened

1 large egg

½ teaspoon vanilla extract

½ cup all-purpose flour

½ teaspoon baking powder

Pinch of salt

¼ teaspoon ground cinnamon

For the ice cream base:

1 (14-ounce) can sweetened condensed milk

1 cup peach preserves (store-bought or home-made), divided

2 cups heavy whipping cream

To make the cobbler: Preheat the oven to 350°F. Line a baking sheet with parchment paper.

In a medium bowl, cream the butter on medium-high speed with an electric mixer. Add the egg and vanilla; mix well. Next, add the flour, baking powder, salt, and cinnamon. Mix until a soft dough forms. Using a cookie scoop, scoop the dough onto the parchment paper about 2 inches apart. Bake 10–12 minutes, or until the cookies are golden brown. Remove from the oven, and let cool completely. Once the cookies are cool, crumble them into small pieces and crumbs.

To make the ice cream base: Stir together the sweetened condensed milk and ½ cup peach preserves in a large bowl. In the bowl of a stand mixer using the whisk attachment, whip the heavy cream on high speed until stiff peaks form. Fold the whipped cream into the sweetened condensed milk mixture.

To prepare: Spoon half of the ice cream base into a 9 × 5-inch loaf pan. Drizzle or dollop with ¼ cup peach preserves. Top with half of the crumbled cookies. Repeat the layers with the remaining ice cream base, peach preserves, and crumbles. Freeze 4–6 hours, or overnight.

lemon-lime icebox cake

This easy icebox cake layers graham crackers, which soften to a cake-like texture while the cake chills in the refrigerator, with homemade lemon-lime custard for a rich and creamy frozen treat.

SERVES 9

For the custard:

4 large egg yolks, lightly beaten

¾ cup granulated sugar

2 tablespoons cornstarch

2 cups whole milk

¼ cup fresh lemon juice

¼ cup fresh lime juice

1 teaspoon vanilla extract

For the whipped cream:

1½ cups heavy whipping cream

3 tablespoons confectioners' sugar

1 teaspoon vanilla extract

For the cake:

3 sleeves graham crackers

To make the custard: Place the egg yolks in a small bowl, and set aside. In a medium saucepan over medium heat, combine the sugar, cornstarch, milk, both juices, and vanilla. Cook, whisking slowly, until the sugar dissolves. The mixture should be thoroughly heated but not boiling. Add about ¼ cup of the mixture to the egg yolks, and whisk quickly to temper the eggs. Immediately add the egg mixture back to the saucepan, and continue whisking quickly to prevent the eggs from scrambling. Whisk until the mixture thickens into the consistency of pudding and coats the back of a rubber spatula or wooden spoon, about 5–10 minutes.

Remove from the heat, and immediately cover the top of the pudding with clear plastic wrap (directly on the surface of the pudding). Poke a few holes in the plastic wrap with a knife. Let the pudding cool at room temperature for about 1 hour. Transfer it to the refrigerator, and chill 2–3 hours, or overnight.

To make the whipped cream: In the bowl of a stand mixer using the whisk attachment, whip the cream, confectioners' sugar, and vanilla on high speed until stiff peaks form.

To assemble the cake: Break the graham crackers into squares. Arrange one layer of crackers in an 8 X 8-inch or 9 X 9-inch square baking dish. Spread with half of the pudding. Add a second layer of graham crackers and pudding. Top with a third layer of graham crackers. Spread the whipped cream over the graham crackers. Chill in the refrigerator 3–4 hours, or overnight.

peach and sweet tea–lemonade floats

No Southern cookbook would be complete without sweet tea, and in this perfect summer recipe, two Southern favorites come together in a twist on an American classic.

MAKES 4

2 cups sweet tea

½ cup lemonade

1 cup club soda

½ gallon vanilla ice cream

Frozen sliced peaches

For the garnishes:

Peach slices

Lemon slices

In a pitcher, stir together the sweet tea, lemonade, and club soda. Fill four glasses with a couple scoops of ice cream. Top with the sweet tea mixture. Garnish with frozen peaches or lemon slices, if desired.

banana pudding trifles
with Spiced Honey Caramel Sauce

This recipes forgoes the box pudding mixes in favor of a homemade banana pudding that gets an extra boost of flavor from caramel sauce sweetened with honey and spiced with cinnamon and nutmeg.

MAKES 6–8

For the spiced honey caramel sauce:

1 cup granulated sugar

6 tablespoons cold butter, diced

¼ cup heavy whipping cream

⅓ cup honey

¼ teaspoon cinnamon

⅛ teaspoon nutmeg

Pinch of salt

For the homemade pudding:

½ cup granulated sugar

3 tablespoons all-purpose flour

Pinch of salt

2 cups whole milk

3 large egg yolks, lightly beaten

1 teaspoon vanilla extract

For the whipped cream:

1 cup heavy whipping cream

3 tablespoons confectioners' sugar

1 teaspoon vanilla extract

For the trifles:

1 box vanilla wafers, crushed

5–6 large bananas, sliced

To make the caramel sauce: Place the sugar in a medium saucepan over medium heat. Stir occasionally until the sugar begins to clump together. Continue cooking until the clumps begin to melt and turn amber in color. Stir occasionally until completely melted. While stirring, add the diced butter a little at a time, stirring quickly to incorporate. Gradually add the cream until incorporated. Reduce the heat to low, and continue cooking for an additional minute. Remove from the heat, and stir in the honey, cinnamon, nutmeg, and salt. Let cool completely before using. (The caramel sauce can be made in advance and kept in a sealed container at room temperature.)

To make the pudding: Combine the sugar, flour, and salt in a large saucepan. Stir together the milk and egg yolks in a medium bowl. Add the milk mixture to the dry ingredients in the saucepan, and cook, stirring constantly, over medium-low heat for 10–15 minutes, or until the mixture is very thick and pudding-like in texture. Remove from the heat, stir in the vanilla, and immediately press a piece of plastic wrap over the surface of the pudding. Let the pudding cool completely.

To make the whipped cream: In the bowl of a stand mixer using the whisk attachment, whip the cream, confectioners' sugar, and vanilla on high speed until stiff peaks form.

To assemble the trifles: Spoon a layer of pudding into the bottom of six to eight cups (the number of servings will vary depending on the size of cups used). Top with crushed vanilla wafers, whipped cream, caramel sauce, and sliced bananas. Repeat the layers if using large cups. Store covered in the refrigerator until ready to serve.

Other southern Favorites

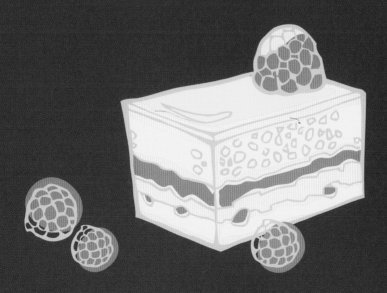

dark chocolate–peanut butter cobbler

No, this is not the fruity kind of cobbler. This indulgent dessert is similar to a sticky cake with a gooey sauce on the bottom. Serve with a dusting of confectioners' sugar and ice cream!

SERVES 8

For the cobbler:

1 cup all-purpose flour

¼ cup Hershey's Special Dark Cocoa Powder

Pinch of ground cinnamon

¾ cup granulated sugar

2 teaspoons baking powder

½ teaspoon salt

¾ cup whole milk

⅓ cup butter, melted

1 tablespoon vanilla extract

⅓ cup creamy peanut butter

½ cup dark chocolate chips

For the topping:

2 tablespoon Hershey's Special Dark Cocoa Powder

½ cup packed light brown sugar

1 cup boiling water

For the garnishes:

Confectioners' sugar

Vanilla ice cream

To make the cobbler: Preheat oven to 350°F. Whisk together the flour, cocoa powder, cinnamon, sugar, baking powder, and salt. Make a well in the center of the dry ingredients, and add the milk, butter, vanilla, and peanut butter. Stir until the ingredients are well blended. Fold in the chocolate chips. Spread the batter in a greased 8-inch baking dish.

To make the topping: Stir together the cocoa powder and brown sugar. Sprinkle evenly over the batter in the pan. Pour the boiling water over the top of the batter, but DO NOT MIX.

To make the cake: Bake 35–40 minutes, or until the top looks crackled and the center is almost set. Remove from the oven, and cool for 15–20 minutes. Serve warm dusted with confectioners' sugar or with a scoop of ice cream, if desired.

Lavender-Lemon Bars

Lavender pairs so wonderfully with lemon that I couldn't resist adding a light floral flavor to these lemon bars! They have a classic shortbread crust and plenty of confectioners' sugar on top.

SERVES 12

For the crust:

1 cup unsalted butter, softened

½ cup granulated sugar

½ teaspoon salt

1 teaspoon vanilla extract

2 cups all-purpose flour

For the lavender-lemon filling:

2½ cups granulated sugar

½ teaspoon dried lavender buds

6 large eggs

1 cup fresh lemon juice

½ teaspoon lavender extract

2 tablespoons lemon zest

For the garnish:

Confectioners' sugar

Lemon zest

Lavender buds

To make the crust: Preheat the oven to 350°F. Spray a 9 × 13-inch pan with cooking spray. Line the pan with parchment paper, leaving a couple of inches of overhang on the sides.

In a large bowl, cream the butter and sugar on medium-high speed with an electric mixer until fluffy. Add the salt, vanilla, and half of the flour. Mix until combined. Add the remaining flour, and mix well. Press the dough into the prepared pan, and bake 20–22 minutes, or until the crust is lightly golden brown around the edges. Remove from the oven.

To make the filling: Combine the sugar and lavender buds in a food processor. Pulse until the lavender is finely ground. Whisk together the sugar mixture, eggs, lemon juice, extract, and lemon zest. Pour the filling over the crust, and carefully return to the oven. Bake for another 30–35 minutes, or until set.

To finish: Let the bars cool completely, then cover them and transfer to the refrigerator. Chill for at least 2 hours, or overnight. When ready to serve, dust with confectioners' sugar and cut into squares.

apple pie milkshakes

These milkshakes just scream fall! Here I have a recipe for apple pie filling, which is then blended with some ice cream and pie crust pieces, but you can always use actual leftover pie if you happen to have some.

MAKES 2–4

For the apple pie filling:

2 cups diced sweet apples

1 tablespoon all-purpose flour

1 teaspoon cinnamon

2 tablespoons packed light brown sugar

For the milkshakes:

1 refrigerated pie crust, thawed

4 cups vanilla ice cream

1½ cups whole milk

1 cup apple pie filling

For the garnishes:

Whipped cream

Apple pie filling

Pie crust

Caramel sauce

To make the apple pie filling: Stir together the apple, flour, cinnamon, and brown sugar in a medium saucepan over medium heat. Cook 10–15 minutes, stirring occasionally, until the apples are soft. Remove from the heat, and let cool completely.

To make the milkshakes: Preheat the oven to 350°F. Line a baking sheet with parchment paper. Unroll the pie crust on a lightly floured surface. Using a pizza cutter, cut the pie crust in half and then into 1-inch strips. Arrange on the baking sheet, and bake 15–18 minutes, or until golden brown. Remove from the oven, and cool completely.

Combine the ice cream, milk, 1 cup apple pie filling, and 6–8 strips of pie crust. Blend until smooth. Pour into cups or jars. Garnish with whipped cream, any remaining apple pie filling, pie crust, and caramel sauce.

butter pecan madeleines

These madeleines are light and airy, like little buttery, pecan-flavored clouds. They're delicious with a cup of coffee and make great additions to holiday tables.

MAKES ABOUT 40

For the madeleines:

⅔ cup granulated sugar

3 large eggs

1 cup all-purpose flour

½ teaspoon baking soda

½ cup butter, melted and cooled

2 teaspoons butter flavoring

½ cup finely chopped pecans

For the garnishes:

Melted white chocolate

Chopped pecans

Preheat the oven to 350°F. Spray two madeleine pans with nonstick cooking spray. Combine the sugar and eggs in a medium bowl, and mix on medium-low speed with an electric mixer until foamy. Next, add the flour and baking soda, and mix until combined. Then add the melted butter and butter flavoring. Fold in the chopped pecans.

Spoon approximately ½ tablespoon of the batter into each of the shell-shaped cavities on the madeleine pans. Bake 8–10 minutes, or until the edges are golden brown and domed in the center.

Let the madeleines cool in the pans for a few minutes, then transfer to a rack to cool completely. Garnish with drizzles of white chocolate and chopped pecans. Store covered at room temperature.

s'mores skillet cookie

Making skillet cookies is my favorite way to do cookies. This one has a graham cracker crust, chunks of chocolate, toasty marshmallows, and that perfect warm, gooey center.

SERVES 8

For the crust:

1½ cups graham cracker crumbs

½ cup butter, melted

For the s'mores cookie dough:

1 cup butter, room temperature

¾ cup granulated sugar

½ cup packed light brown sugar

2 large eggs

1 teaspoon vanilla extract

1 teaspoon salt

1 teaspoon baking soda

2¼ cups all-purpose flour

2 cups chocolate chunks

For the topping:

1 cup mini marshmallows

To make the crust: Preheat the oven to 350°F. Grease a 9-inch cast-iron skillet with butter or oil. Combine the graham cracker crumbs and melted butter in a medium bowl, stirring until the crumbs are evenly coated. Press the mixture into the bottom of the skillet. Bake for 10 minutes, then remove from the oven.

To make the cookie dough: In a large bowl, cream the butter on medium speed with an electric mixer until smooth. Add both sugars, and mix until fluffy. Add the eggs and vanilla; mix well. Add the salt, baking soda, and flour. Mix on low speed until mostly combined and then on medium speed until completely combined. Fold in the chocolate chunks.

To assemble: Carefully press the dough over the crust in the skillet. Bake 25–28 minutes, or until the cookie is golden brown.

Remove the skillet from the oven, and turn the oven to broil. Arrange the mini marshmallows on top of the cookie. Return the skillet to the oven, and let the marshmallows toast for about 30 seconds, or until golden brown. Marshmallows burn easily, so make sure to watch carefully while toasting.

Let the skillet cookie cool slightly; cut into wedges and serve warm.

bourbon-pecan pie-stuffed baked apples

If you're going to stuff and fill fruit for dessert, you might as well go all out! These apples are filled with pecan pie filling and a splash of bourbon.

MAKES 6

For the filling:

½ cup light corn syrup

1 large egg

⅓ cup granulated sugar

1 tablespoon butter, melted

½ teaspoon vanilla extract

¼ teaspoon cinnamon

2 tablespoons bourbon

1 cup chopped pecans

For the apples:

6 Honey Crisp apples

1 cup water, apple juice,
  or apple cider

For the garnish:

Ice cream

For the filling: Combine the corn syrup, egg, sugar, butter, vanilla, cinnamon, and bourbon in a medium bowl. Whisk to combine, and stir in the pecans.

For the apples: Preheat the oven to 375°F. Gently scrub the apples in hot water to remove any waxy coating. Remove the cores from the apples with a sharp knife or melon baller, leaving about ½ inch at the bottom. Fill the apples with the pecan pie filling, and place in a 9 × 13-inch pan. Pour the water, juice, or cider into the pan.

Bake for 20 minutes, then cover the pan loosely with aluminum foil to prevent the pecans from burning. Bake for another 40 minutes. Remove the pan from the oven, and let cool. Serve warm with a scoop of ice cream.

strawberry buttermilk doughnuts

Thanks to the buttermilk and fresh strawberries, these doughnuts are moist, cakey, and perfectly enjoyable all summer long.

MAKES 12–14 DOUGHNUTS

For the strawberry buttermilk doughnuts:

4 cups all-purpose flour

2 teaspoons baking soda

1 teaspoon salt

3 large eggs

1 cup granulated sugar

1 cup buttermilk

¼ cup butter, melted

2 teaspoons vanilla extract

1½ cups chopped fresh strawberries

Vegetable oil, for frying

For the strawberry glaze:

1 (1-ounce) package freeze-dried strawberries

1 cup confectioners' sugar

3–4 tablespoons whole milk

To make the doughnuts: Whisk together the flour, baking soda, and salt in a medium bowl; set aside. In a large bowl, beat the eggs on medium speed with an electric mixer until frothy. Add the sugar; mix well. Add the milk, melted butter, and vanilla. Add half of the flour mixture; mix until combined. Repeat with the remaining flour. Fold in the chopped strawberries. Cover the bowl, and let the dough sit in the refrigerator for about 30 minutes.

Roll out the dough on a well-floured surface to about a ¾-inch thickness. (It can be helpful to work with portions of the dough, and not all of the dough at once. Chilled dough is easier to work with, so feel free to roll out half and leave the other half in the refrigerator.) Using a 3- or 4-inch round cookie cutter, cut circles out of the dough. Use a ½-inch or 1-inch cutter to cut holes in the middle of each doughnut.

Fill a heavy-bottomed pot with 2 inches of oil, and heat to 360°F. Fry 3 or 4 doughnuts at a time, cooking for 3–4 minutes, or until golden brown. Flip and cook for another 3–4 minutes. Use a metal slotted spoon to remove the doughnuts and transfer them to a wire rack placed on top of several sheets of paper towels. Repeat with the remaining dough. Let the doughnuts cool completely before glazing.

To make the glaze: Process the freeze-dried strawberries in a food processor until finely ground. Whisk together the processed strawberries, confectioners' sugar, and milk until smooth. Dip the doughnuts in the glaze, and return them to the wire rack to let the glaze set.

butterscotch brownies

This is one of my favorite recipes from my grandmother's recipe collection. It uses butterscotch chips instead of chocolate chips to make the perfect gooey brownies with creamy butterscotch frosting.

SERVES 8

For the brownies:

1¼ cups butterscotch morsels, divided

4 tablespoons butter

1 cup packed light brown sugar

2 large eggs

1 teaspoon vanilla extract

1 cup all-purpose flour

1 teaspoon baking powder

1 teaspoon salt

For the frosting:

1 cup butter, softened

1 teaspoon vanilla extract

3 tablespoons butterscotch morsels, melted and cooled

4 cups confectioners' sugar

For the garnishes:

Butterscotch chips

Sprinkles

To make the brownies: Preheat the oven to 350°F. Spray an 8 X 8-inch baking dish with cooking spray.

Combine 1 cup butterscotch morsels and the butter in a microwave-safe dish. Heat in 30-second intervals, stirring well between each, until melted and smooth. Stir in the brown sugar until well blended. Add the eggs and vanilla; stir well. Next, fold in the flour, baking powder, and salt. Spread the batter in the prepared pan. Sprinkle with the remaining ¼ cup butterscotch chips. Bake 35 minutes. Remove from the oven, and allow to cool completely before frosting.

To make the frosting: In a medium bowl, cream the butter on medium-high speed with an electric mixer until smooth. Add the vanilla and melted butterscotch; mix well. Add half of the confectioners' sugar, and mix until incorporated. Repeat with the second half of the confectioners' sugar.

To make the brownies: Spread the frosting over the cooled brownies, and top with extra butterscotch chips or sprinkles.

apple-pear fritters

Fresh apples and pears were meant for fritters! These fritters are light and pillowy on the inside and nice and golden brown on the outside.

MAKES 18–20 FRITTERS

2½ cups all-purpose flour

⅓ cup granulated sugar

2 teaspoons baking powder

¼ teaspoon ground cinnamon

Pinch of ground nutmeg

1 teaspoon salt

2 large eggs

1 teaspoon vanilla extract

¾ cup whole milk

2 tablespoons vegetable oil

1½ cups peeled, chopped sweet apples (such as Honey Crisp)

1½ cups peeled, chopped sweet pears (such as Bartlett)

Vegetable oil, for frying

Confectioners' sugar, for dusting

In a medium bowl, whisk together the flour, sugar, baking powder, cinnamon, nutmeg, and salt. In another medium bowl, whisk together the eggs, vanilla, milk, and oil. Add the milk mixture to the flour mixture, and gently fold until combined. Fold in the apples and pears.

Heat 2 inches of oil in a heavy-bottom pot over medium-high heat until a candy thermometer reaches 350°F. Place a wire rack over several layers of paper on the counter nearby.

Using a cookie scoop, drop the batter into the hot oil, cooking about 4 or 5 fritters at a time. Let the fritters cook 3–4 minutes on both sides until they are golden brown. Remove with a slotted spoon, and transfer to the wire rack. Repeat as necessary for remaining fritter batter. Once the fritters have cooled slightly, dust them with confectioners' sugar.

birthday buttermilk biscuits

I was inspired to make these biscuits after having something similar at Callie's Hot Little Biscuit in Charleston. Warm, buttery biscuits with pops of color and sweet glaze are the perfect Southern treat!

MAKES 12

For the biscuits:

2 cups all-purpose flour (plus more for dusting)

2 tablespoons granulated sugar

1 tablespoon plus 1 teaspoon baking powder

1 teaspoon salt

½ cup cold butter

1 teaspoon vanilla extract

¾ cup buttermilk

¾ cup rainbow jimmies

¼ cup melted butter

For the maple–vanilla bean glaze:

1½ cups confectioners' sugar

1 vanilla bean, split, with seeds scraped out and reserved

2 tablespoons pure maple syrup

1–2 tablespoons whole milk

For the garnish:

Sprinkles

To make the biscuits: Preheat the oven to 450°F. In a large bowl, whisk together the flour, sugar, baking powder, and salt. Using a box grater, grate the butter onto a piece of parchment paper. Add the butter to the flour mixture, and use a pastry cutter to blend until the mixture is crumbly. Stir in the vanilla and buttermilk until a dough forms.

Turn out the dough onto a well-floured surface. Pat into a 1-inch-thick rectangle. Dust with additional flour, and sprinkle with ½ cup sprinkles. Fold the dough in half, and pat back into a 1-inch-thick rectangle. Repeat this folding process six to eight times. Use a biscuit cutter or 3-inch round cookie cutter to cut out the biscuits.

Arrange the biscuits in a greased 8-inch baking dish. Brush the tops with melted butter. Bake 12–15 minutes, or until puffed and golden brown. Remove from the oven, and let cool.

To make the glaze: Combine the confectioners' sugar, vanilla bean seeds, maple syrup, and milk in a medium bowl. Whisk until smooth.

To serve: Serve the glaze over warm biscuits and garnish with sprinkles.

red velvet moon pies®

The South's favorite sandwich cookie meets the South's most colorful cake! Red velvet is a personal favorite of mine, so red velvet moon pies® seemed like a natural spin to put on these cookies.

MAKES 10–12 MOON PIES

For the red velvet cookies:

2½ cups all-purpose flour

1 tablespoon unsweetened cocoa powder

½ teaspoon baking soda

½ teaspoon salt

1 cup butter, softened

1½ cups granulated sugar

2 large eggs

1 teaspoon vanilla extract

1 teaspoon white vinegar

1 tablespoon red gel food coloring

For the marshmallow filling:

¾ cup light corn syrup

1 cup granulated sugar

3 large egg whites

½ teaspoon cream of tartar

1 teaspoon vanilla extract

For the chocolate coating:

1 (12-ounce) package dark chocolate chips

¼ cup vegetable oil

For the garnish:

Sprinkles

To make the cookies: Whisk together the flour, cocoa powder, baking soda, and salt in a medium bowl. Set aside. In a large bowl, cream the butter on medium-high speed with an electric mixer until smooth. Add the sugar, and mix until fluffy. Add the eggs and vanilla; mix well. Mix in the vinegar. Add the flour mixture, and mix on low until mostly combined, then on medium until completely combined. Add the food coloring, and mix until well blended. Refrigerate for 30 minutes.

When ready to bake the cookies, preheat the oven to 350°F. Line two baking sheets with parchment paper. Using a cookie scoop, drop dough 2 inches apart on the prepared baking sheets, about 6–8 per baking sheet. Bake 9–10 minutes, or until the cookies are firm around the edges and still a little soft in the middle. Remove from the oven, and allow to cool for a few minutes. Transfer to a wire rack to cool completely. Repeat with remaining dough.

To make the marshmallow filling: Combine the corn syrup and sugar in a small saucepan over medium-high heat. Clip a candy thermometer to the side of the pan, and bring the mixture to a simmer. While the syrup mixture is heating, combine the egg whites and cream of tartar in the bowl of a stand mixer fitted with the whisk attachment. Whip the egg whites until soft peaks form. When the candy thermometer reaches 240°F, remove from the heat. With the mixer running, carefully pour the syrup in a steady stream into the egg whites. Continue whipping until the mixture is thick, glossy, and stiff peaks form. Mix in the vanilla. Transfer the marshmallow filling to a piping bag. Pipe the filling onto half of the cookies; top with the remaining cookies.

To make the chocolate coating: Place the chocolate and oil in a microwave-safe dish. Microwave in 30-second intervals, stirring well between each, until smooth. Dip the moon pies in chocolate, or gently spoon it over the top. Garnish with sprinkles. Let the chocolate set before serving.

maple apple butter crumb bars

Here is my Southern version of crumb bars! This homemade apple butter is flavored with maple syrup and is wonderful paired with the buttery crumbs. These bars are a nice breakfast treat or afternoon snack.

SERVES 9

For the apple butter:

4 cups chopped apple (such as Honey Crisp or Gala)

½ cup packed light brown sugar

⅓ cup pure maple syrup

1 teaspoon maple extract (optional)

1 teaspoon cinnamon

¼ teaspoon nutmeg

¼ cup apple juice

1 teaspoon vanilla extract

For the crumb:

1½ cups all-purpose flour

⅔ cup sugar

½ teaspoon salt

¼ teaspoon baking powder

½ teaspoon cinnamon

½ cup butter, cubed

½ cup old-fashioned oats

To make the filling: Place the apples in a blender, and blend until smooth. Add the apple puree, brown sugar, maple syrup, maple extract, cinnamon, nutmeg, apple juice, and vanilla to a medium saucepan over medium-low heat. Cook, stirring occasionally, until the mixture is thick and resembles the consistency of jam, about 1 hour to 1 hour and 30 minutes. Mixture should hold its shape when spread. Remove from the heat, and let cool completely. (Apple butter can be made a day or two in advance and stored in a sealed container in the refrigerator.)

To make the crumb: Preheat the oven to 350°F. Spray an 8 X 8-inch baking dish with cooking spray. Combine all of the crumb ingredients in a food processor. Pulse until the dough begins to come together but is still crumbly. Remove 2 ½ cups, and press into the bottom of the baking dish. Bake 15 minutes, and remove from the oven. Spread the apple butter evenly over the crust. Sprinkle the remaining crumbs evenly over the apple butter. Bake 25–30 minutes, or until the crumb mixture is golden brown. Let the bars cool in the pan before cutting into squares.

chocolate-cherry crumble ice cream cake

Reminiscent of Black Forest cake, this ice cream cake has layers of chocolate ice cream, crunchy chocolate cookies, ganache, and homemade cherry sauce.

SERVES 8–10

For the cherry sauce:

4 cups pitted cherries

1 cup granulated sugar

Juice of 1 lemon

½ cup plus 2 tablespoons water, divided

1 tablespoon cornstarch

1 teaspoon vanilla extract

For the chocolate ganache:

1 (12-ounce) package semi-sweet chocolate chips

1¼ cups heavy whipping cream

For the ice cream cake:

1 (48-ounce) carton chocolate ice cream, thawed

1 (9-ounce) package chocolate wafer cookies, crushed

To make the cherry sauce: Combine the cherries, sugar, lemon juice, and ½ cup water in a medium saucepan over medium heat. Bring the mixture to a simmer, and cook, stirring occasionally, until the cherries begin to break down and the sugar has dissolved, about 10 minutes. In a separate bowl, stir together the 2 tablespoons water and the cornstarch; add to the saucepan. Continue cooking, stirring occasionally, until the mixture thickens and resembles syrup, about 10–12 minutes. Remove from the heat and stir in the vanilla. Let the syrup cool completely.

To make the ganache: Combine the chocolate chips and cream in a medium saucepan over medium-low heat. Stirring slowly but constantly, cook until the chocolate melts and the mixture is smooth. Remove from the heat, and let cool completely.

To make the ice cream cake: Line a 9 × 5-inch loaf pan with parchment paper, leaving an overhang on two sides. (The overhang will be used to lift the ice cream cake out of the pan once frozen.) Spoon a layer of ice cream into the bottom of the loaf pan, and smooth with the back of a spoon. Sprinkle a layer of crushed cookies over the ice cream, drizzle with ganache, and then add the sauce. Repeat the layers a second time. Freeze 3–4 hours, or until the ice cream is firm. Run a hot knife around the edges of the pan to loosen. Lift the ice cream cake from the pan by gripping the parchment overhang, and cut into slices to serve.

giant orange sweet roll

I've never been a huge fan of orange-flavored sweets, except when it comes to orange sweet rolls, which my grandmother would make on occasion when she watched my cousins and me during the summers. Cut this giant version into wedges and enjoy!

SERVES 8

For the dough:

3 cups all-purpose flour, divided

¼ cup granulated sugar

½ teaspoon salt

2¼ teaspoons instant yeast

½ cup warm water

⅓ cup whole milk

¼ cup butter

1 large egg, lightly beaten

For the filling:

4 tablespoons butter, very soft

1 cup orange jam or marmalade

½ cup packed light brown sugar

½ teaspoon ground cardamom (optional)

For the orange glaze:

1½ cups confectioners' sugar

3–4 tablespoons orange juice

1 tablespoon orange zest

To make the dough: In a large bowl, whisk together the flour, sugar, salt, and instant yeast. In a medium saucepan over medium-low heat, combine the water, milk, and butter. Stirring slowly, cook until the butter melts and the mixture is thoroughly heated. Remove from the heat, and stir into the flour mixture. Add the egg, and stir until the dough begins to pull away from the sides of the bowl. Cover with plastic wrap, and let rise in a warm, dry place for 1 hour.

To assemble the sweet roll: Turn the dough onto a lightly floured surface. Roll out the dough into a large rectangle. Spread the dough with butter and marmalade. Evenly sprinkle brown sugar over the marmalade; then sprinkle with cardamom, if using. Using a pizza cutter, cut the dough into 2-inch strips. Starting with one strip of dough, begin at one end and roll up. Place in the center of a lightly greased 9-inch round baking dish. Continue wrapping strips of dough around and around. When all the dough has been used, there will still be space left in the pan. Loosely cover the pan with plastic wrap, and let it rise in a warm, draft-free place for 1 ½–2 hours. (You can turn on the oven light—do not turn on the oven—and place the pan in the oven to rise.)

Once the dough has doubled in size, remove the pan from the oven, and preheat the oven to 350°F. Bake the roll 30–35 minutes. Remove from the oven and cool slightly.

To make the glaze: Whisk together the confectioners' sugar, orange juice, and zest. Drizzle the glaze over the sweet roll. Cut into wedges to serve.

ambrosia bars

These bars are a cool and creamy version of the popular Southern fruit salad often enjoyed as a side dish or dessert. Almost like a no-bake pie, these bars have a graham cracker crust and are definitely meant for dessert.

SERVES 8–10

For the crust:

1½ cups graham cracker crumbs

6 tablespoons coconut oil, melted

For the filling:

1 (8-ounce) package cream cheese

1 (6-ounce) container plain Greek yogurt

1 teaspoon vanilla extract

½ tablespoon orange zest

1½ cups heavy whipping cream

1½ cups mini marshmallows

1 cup shredded coconut

For the toppings:

1 cup cubed pineapple

1 cup orange segments

1 cup maraschino cherries, halved

¼ cup shredded coconut

¼ cup chopped pecans

To make the crust: Preheat the oven to 350°F. Line an 8- or 9-inch square baking dish with aluminum foil. Lightly mist with cooking spray.

In a medium bowl, stir together the graham cracker crumbs and coconut oil, and press the crust into the prepared pan. Bake 12 minutes; remove from the oven, and cool completely.

To make the filling: In a large bowl, beat the cream cheese on medium speed with an electric mixer until smooth. Add the yogurt, vanilla, and orange zest; mix well. In a separate medium bowl, whip the heavy cream on high speed until stiff peaks form. Fold into the cream cheese mixture. Fold in the marshmallows and coconut.

To assemble: Spread the filling over the cooled crust in the pan. Arrange the topping ingredients over the filling, and press down slightly. Loosely cover, and chill 4–6 hours in the refrigerator.

butter pecan biscuit bread pudding

This bread pudding forgoes traditional bread and uses southern-style buttermilk biscuits instead! It's sprinkled with chopped pecans and covered with a bourbon–brown sugar sauce.

SERVES 6–8

For the biscuits:

2 cups all-purpose flour (plus more for dusting)

2 tablespoons granulated sugar

1 tablespoon plus 1 teaspoon baking powder

1 teaspoon salt

½ cup plus 2 tablespoons cold butter

1 teaspoon butter flavoring

1 cup buttermilk

2 tablespoons chopped pecans

For the bread pudding:

6 cups cubed biscuits

2 cups whole milk

4 tablespoons butter, melted

¾ cup granulated sugar

4 large eggs

1 teaspoon vanilla extract

½ teaspoon cinnamon

¼ teaspoon nutmeg

½ cup chopped pecans

For the brown sugar–bourbon sauce:

¼ cup butter

½ cup packed light brown sugar

¼ cup heavy whipping cream

¼ cup bourbon

To make the biscuits: Preheat the oven to 450°F. In a large bowl, whisk together the flour, sugar, baking powder, and salt. Using a box grater, grate the ½ cup butter onto a piece of parchment paper. Add the butter to the flour mixture, and use a pastry cutter to blend until the mixture is crumbly. Stir in the butter flavoring and buttermilk until a dough forms.

Turn out the dough onto a well-floured surface. Pat into a 1-inch-thick rectangle. Dust with flour, and sprinkle with the 2 tablespoons pecans. Fold the dough in half, and pat back into a 1-inch-thick rectangle. Repeat this process six to eight times. Use a biscuit cutter or 3-inch round cookie cutter to cut out the biscuits.

Arrange the biscuits in a lightly greased 8- or 9-inch baking dish. Melt the remaining 2 tablespoons of butter in a small saucepan over medium heat and brush onto tops of buscuits. Bake 12–15 minutes, or until puffed and golden brown. Remove from the oven. Once the biscuits are cool, cut into 1-inch cubes.

To make the bread pudding: Preheat the oven to 350°F. Spray a 9 X 9-inch baking dish with cooking spray. Arrange the cubed biscuits in an even layer in the dish. Whisk together the milk, butter, sugar, eggs, vanilla, cinnamon, and nutmeg in a medium bowl. Pour over the biscuits. Sprinkle with pecans. Bake 35–40 minutes, or until lightly golden brown on top. Remove from the oven.

To make the sauce: Melt the butter in a small saucepan over medium heat. Add the brown sugar, cream, and bourbon. Bring the mixture to a boil, and cook, stirring constantly, for 4–5 minutes, or until the consistency resembles a thick syrup or glaze. Remove from the heat. Serve with the bread pudding.

essential crusts

all-butter pie crust

1½ cups all-purpose flour

2 tablespoons granulated
sugar

½ teaspoon salt

6 tablespoons cold butter

6 tablespoons cold water

1 large egg

1 tablespoon whole milk

To make the pie crust, combine the flour, sugar, and salt in a food processor. Add the butter, and pulse until crumbly. With the processor running, add water 1 tablespoon at a time until the dough comes together and forms a ball. Turn out the dough onto a sheet of plastic wrap, and shape into a disc. Chill for 30 minutes.

On a lightly floured surface, turn out the dough, and roll into a 12-inch circle. Lift the dough using a rolling pin (if the dough is hard to work with, return it to the refrigerator to help it firm up a bit), and lay it over a lightly greased 9-inch pie plate. Gently press the dough into the pie plate, and flute the edges.

Beat the egg and milk with a fork until pale and frothy. Brush the egg wash over the edges of the pie crust.

double pie crust

3 cups all-purpose flour

3 tablespoons granulated
   sugar

½ teaspoon salt

½ cup cold butter, diced

¼ cup vegetable shortening

½ cup cold water

To make the double pie crust, combine the flour, sugar, and salt in a food processor. Add the butter and shortening, and pulse until crumbly. With the processor running, add water 1 tablespoon at a time until the dough comes together and forms a ball. Divide the dough into two balls, shape into discs, and wrap with plastic wrap. Chill in the refrigerator 30 minutes.

index

about the author

Beth Branch was born and raised in Birmingham, Alabama. She began baking and created her first food blog, *The Collegiate Baker*, in 2011 while she was a student at the University of Alabama. Her early baking adventures mainly focused on creating over-the-top birthday cakes for her friends and family, but also included plenty of forays into old family recipes and her grandmother's recipe box. After graduating from college, Branch rebranded her blog as *bethcakes*, the name her friends coined for her over-the-top cakes. In addition to family favorite southern recipes, Branch also plays with modern food trends to create fun recipes for people of all baking experience levels to enjoy.